Ricardo Palma

Twayne's World Authors Series

Luis Davila, Editor of Latin American Literature

TWAS 593

RICARDO PALMA *in 1910*
(1833-1919)

Ricardo Palma

By Merlin D. Compton

Brigham Young University

Twayne Publishers · Boston

Ricardo Palma

Merlin D. Compton

Copyright © 1982 by G.K. Hall & Company
Published by Twayne Publishers
A Division of G.K. Hall & Company
70 Lincoln Street
Boston, Massachusetts 02111

Book design by Barbara Anderson

Printed on permanent / durable acid-free
paper and bound in The United States of
America.

Library of Congress Cataloging in Publication Data

Compton, Merlin D., 1924-
Ricardo Palma.

(Twayne's world author series; TWAS 593)
Bibliography: p. 161
Includes index.
1. Palma, Ricardo, 1833-1919—Criticism and
interpretation. I. Title. II. Series
PQ8497. P26Z63   863   81-7163
ISBN 0-8057-6435-6   AACR2

Contents

About the Author

Merlin D. Compton was born in Ogden, Utah, in 1924. He served in the United States Army Air Force from 1943–1946 during the Second World War. In 1952 he graduated from Brigham Young University with a B.A.; he took his M.A. from the same institution in 1954 and in 1959 he graduated from the University of California, Los Angeles, with his Ph.D. in Hispanic Languages and Literature. Professor Compton has served on the faculties of Adams State College (Colorado), Weber State College (Utah), and Brigham Young University, where he is a professor of Spanish and Portuguese.

Showing an early interest in the writings of Ricardo Palma, Professor Compton wrote a doctoral dissertation entitled "Spanish Honor in the *Tradiciones Peruanas* of Ricardo Palma." He has since published three monographs on Palma—one in the *Duquesne Hispanic Review* (Spring 1969) and two in *Fénix* (No. 23, 1973). In 1978 Professor Compton did research on Palma in the National Library in Lima, Peru, where he was able to work with Palma's private collection.

Professor Compton is married to the former Avon Allen; they are the parents of five children, two of whom are married.

Preface

Although virtually every student of Hispanic literature has sampled the writings of Ricardo Palma, most English speakers are unaware of this outstanding writer. Only a small number of his "tradiciones" (short prose pieces combining fact and fiction) are available in English translation and there are no works in English which treat in depth either his life or his works. It is the purpose of this book to fill this gap and make it possible for Americans and others who speak English to become acquainted with a significant Peruvian and his works. At the same time this volume will provide in one place information about Palma and his works which the serious student of Spanish American literature will find useful.

Ricardo Palma, politician, library director, and man of letters, left his imprint on Peru in a number of ways, but his principal contribution was his *Tradiciones peruanas.* They were popular as soon as the first collection of "tradiciones" was published in 1872 and new editions continue to be printed. The literary world is much richer because of the labors of this writer, whose influence spread far and whose "tradiciones" many attempted to imitate, but without success. His works constitute a scintillating magic carpet which carries us into a fascinating period which would now be mummified and forgotten were it not for the pen of a man who buried his life in the past in order that the Peru of old could be infused with life.

During his lifetime Ricardo Palma published more than five hundred "tradiciones," five collections of poetry, several historical works, two works on lexicography, two memoirs, and many other works. In addition he wrote for newspapers and magazines, composed some dramas, penned hundreds of revealing letters, wrote many prologues to literary works, and prepared numerous articles of literary criticism.

Chapter 1 treats Palma's life and times; Chapters 2 and 3 provide information about the "tradición," its nature and development;

Chapter 4 deals with the flavor of the "tradiciones," that is to say, life in old Peru as seen in these pieces; Chapter 5 treats his lesser works; and Chapter 6 deals with the influence of Palma on other writers and his importance in the literary world.

I have chosen not to study Palma's "Tradiciones en salsa verde" because the somewhat salacious nature of many of these pieces makes them unsuitable for a book of this kind, and I have given his dramas little attention, not because they are not important but because only one of them survived the playwright's attempts to destroy all of his dramas. I felt that it would be unwise to try to study his theater with any degree of seriousness under these circumstances. And finally, some readers may feel that I have not given Palma's poetry the attention it deserves. To them I would say that Palma's reputation is based on his "tradiciones." My study of his verses serves two principal purposes: first, to show how his prose and poetry developed in a parallel fashion, and second, to provide additional information about his personality and aesthetic attitudes, especially during the early years of his career, a period during which our information about Palma is sketchy. His poetry deserves a more complete study but it lies outside the scope of this work.

The principal collection of "tradiciones" I have used is *Tradiciones peruanas completas* edited by Edith Palma. It is the second edition and was published in Madrid in 1953 by Aguilar. References to it in the body of this work will be indicated by the name of the publisher, "Aguilar." The principal collection of Palma's poetry I have used is *Poesías completas* [Complete Poems], published in Barcelona in 1911. References to it in the body of this work will be made by using the title *Poesías completas*.

All translations are mine.

Merlin D. Compton

Brigham Young University

Acknowledgments

Special acknowledgment is made to Brigham Young University for providing some of the funds for the typing of the manuscript and to Dr. M. Carl Gibson, Chairman of the Department of Spanish and Portuguese, without whose cooperation this book would have taken much longer to complete. Special thanks are expressed to my colleague Dr. Thomas E. Lyon for reading the manuscript and making many valuable critical suggestions. And finally, my deep appreciation to William Wilder, who provided me with materials on Palma I would not have been able to locate through my own resources. His dissertation and other works dealing with Palma which he sent me furnished the incentive for continuing to study the life and works of Ricardo Palma.

Chronology

1833   February 7: Ricardo Palma (christened Manuel Palma) born in Lima, Peru, natural son of Pedro Palma and Dominga Soriano.

1848   Publishes his first verses in *El Comercio* and is director of the satirical newspaper *El Diablo* [The Devil].

1851   Presents his first play, *La hermana del verdugo* [The Executioner's Sister], and his second, *La muerte o la libertad* [Death or Liberty]. Publishes another play, *Rodil*, and his first extant short narrative piece, "Consolación."

1852   Presents *Rodil*. Is appointed a naval officer. Collaborates on the satirical newspaper *El Burro*.

1860   Under the influence of a young revolutionary, José Gálvez, Palma helps storm the home of President Castilla. The attempt fails and the young writer is exiled to Chile.

1861   Moves in literary circles in Chile. Publishes in the *Revista del Pacífico* and the *Revista de Sud América*.

1863   Amnesty is decreed and Palma returns to Peru. Publishes historical work, *Anales de la Inquisición de Lima* [Annals of the Inquisition in Lima].

1864   Travels to Europe, visiting Le Havre, Paris, and London.

1865   Publishes *Armonías* and *Lira americana* in Paris. Editor of *El Mercurio*.

1867   Supports Colonel José Balta in successful revolution against President Mariano Prado. Principal editor of satirical newspaper *La Campana* [The Bell].

1868   Named private secretary to Balta. Named senator from the district of Loreto.

1870	Publishes *Pasionarias* [Passionflowers], Le Havre.
1872	Publishes first series of *Tradiciones.* Balta assassinated in uprising against the government. Palma, disillusioned, retires from politics.
1874	Second series of *Tradiciones.*
1875	Third series of *Tradiciones.*
1876	Marries Cristina Román.
1877	Fourth series of *Tradiciones.* Publishes *Monteagudo y Sánchez Carrión,* historical work which brought down on his head showers of abuse. Publishes more poetry, *Verbos y gerundios* [Verbs and Present Participles]. Collaborates with others in the founding of *La Broma* [The Joke], another satirical newspaper.
1878	*La Broma* ceases publication. Palma named corresponding member of the Royal Spanish Academy.
1879	Chile declares war on Peru and the War of the Pacific begins.
1880	Takes up arms against the invaders in the defense of Miraflores, suburb of Lima, in which he had settled.
1881	His private library is destroyed when his home is razed during the hostilities.
1883	Offered the position of editor of *La Prensa* [The Press], newspaper in Buenos Aires, but refuses the offer when the government persuades him to stay in Peru and undertake the task of rebuilding the National Library, which had been sacked by Chilean soldiers. Publishes *El Demonio de los Andes* [The Demon of the Andes] in New York.
1886	Publishes *Refutación a un compendio de Historia del Perú* [Refutation of a Compendium of a History of Peru].
1889	Publishes *Ropa vieja* [Old Clothes], seventh series of *Tradiciones.*

1890	Publishes first foreign edition of *Tradiciones* in Buenos Aires.
1891	Publishes *Ropa apolillada* [Moth-eaten Clothes], eighth series of *Tradiciones*.
1892	Travels to Spain to represent Peru during the Fourth Centenary of the Discovery of America. Publishes *Filigranas* [Filigrees].
1893	Visits Havana, Cuba, while returning to Peru. Publishes his first edition of *Tradiciones* in Spain (Barcelona, Montaner y Simón, publisher).
1896	*Neologismos y americanismos.*
1899	Ninth series, *Tradiciones y artículos históricos.*
1900	*Cachivaches* [Odds and Ends].
1903	*Papeletas lexicográficas* [Lexicographic Problems].
1906	*Mis últimas tradiciones peruanas* [My Last Peruvian Tradiciones].
1910	*Apéndice a mis últimas tradiciones peruanas* [Appendix to My Last Peruvian Tradiciones].
1911	Death of Cristina, his wife.
1912	His son Clemente loses his position as curator of the library because of his attacks against the government in a periodical. When Palma is not permitted to select Clemente's successor, he resigns. Named in his stead is the caustic Manuel González Prada.
1914	The government is overthrown and Palma is named honorary director of the library by the new government.
1915	Publishes his last "tradición," "Una visita al mariscal Santa Cruz" [A Visit to Marshal Santa Cruz].
1919	Dies at Miraflores, October 6.

Chapter One

The Life and Times of Ricardo Palma

Peru after Independence

The Peru into which Ricardo Palma was born had been free from Spain's domination for fewer than ten years. After the battle of Ayacucho on December 9, 1824, in which the Spanish forces suffered the definitive defeat of the wars for independence, Peru attempted to establish a government patterned along the lines of the one in the United States. However, until 1845, when Ramón Castilla was named president by the Congress, one government after another was overthrown in a country where disorder and instability were the norm. Between the years 1824 and 1845 Peru had seen nine presidents, some of whom had gained the position through constitutional means while others had placed themselves in power by military takeovers. Just when it appeared that Peru would never know a period when it would be governed by constitutional law Castilla appeared on the scene and completely changed the situation in the country.

Having been a prisoner of war in Bolivia, he began to campaign in Arica, where he disembarked with a mere five men. He fought a skirmish there and left the city with his five men, who quickly grew to fifty and later to two hundred. Joined by other military units, Castilla defeated the government troops at San Antonio by out-maneuvering General Guarda. Castilla then pursued Manuel Ignacio Vivanco, the president at that time, until the two forces met in battle near the shores of the Chili River. In that conflict Vivanco was routed and then boarded a ship for Chile.

Ramón Castilla was president of Peru from 1845 to 1863, except for a period of four years when José Rufino Echenique was president. Thus, Castilla became president when Ricardo Palma was twelve years old, and gave up the position when the future literary figure was twenty-nine. During all of Palma's formative years, therefore, except for the period between 1851 and 1854, he was to know only one president, a man whom he considered a dictator when he was young, but who rose in stature in Palma's opinion as the latter grew older and was able to view those turbulent years with more objectivity.

These years are very significant ones in the development of the writer; unfortunately our information concerning them is very limited. During this period Palma spent most of his time attending school, writing poetry and dramas, talking with friends about political and literary matters, and involving himself in newspaper activities. The fact that Castilla was president from the time Palma was twelve until he was twenty-nine (except for a period of four years) caused the writer to look upon Castilla as a dictator and moved him in the direction of liberalism. His poetry and his drama show some evidence of this attitude as will be seen later. His newspaper activities, yet to be studied in depth, present the picture of a young man who chafed under Castilla's seemingly authoritarian regime and longed for the total freedom Romantics dreamed about. Such a detailed study is made difficult because many of these early newspapers have disappeared and because many articles Palma wrote appeared under pen names or with no name at all. Undoubtedly Castilla's administration helped to push Palma in the direction of opposition to what he considered authoritarianism and arbitrary rule. When we add his Romanticism to his reaction against Castilla we can understand why he became a political activist and why he later criticized and mocked authoritarianism whether he found it in the viceroyalty, the Catholic Church, dictatorships or republican governments.

As Palma became more involved with the political affairs of his country and was more able to appreciate the difficulties Castilla had to face, the more his dislike for him changed to a more positive attitude. When Palma saw the turbulence that beset Peru in 1872 with its revolutions, its murders and other horrors, he must have reevaluated the way Castilla had governed, coming to the conclusion that a strong president was imperative in order to maintain order in a country where chaos had reigned for twenty years prior to Castilla's presidency. Perhaps it is a coincidence, but it is about the same year, 1872, that Palma's Romanticism began to wane in a noticeable way. He eliminated to a great degree the outward trappings of Romanticism—the overly sentimental, the clichés, the emphasis on Nature, melodramatic plots, etc.—nevertheless, as a Romantic deep in his soul, he sought his inspiration in his country's past, which he thoroughly enjoyed, and which he could present through the eyes of a Romantic historian, deformed and humorous, but alive and vigorous.

Literary Trends in Peru

Romanticism, which was to hold sway during the greater part of the nineteenth century in Peru, made its entrance in an almost unobtrusive manner. The first writer worthy of note whose works demonstrated some Romantic tendencies was Mariano Melgar (1791–1815), a poet born in Arequipa. Although he was educated in Neoclassicism and translated Virgil and Ovid, his temperament and his role in historical events mark him as a pre-Romantic. Characteristic of his poetry is a vaguely sentimental and complaining note which has a Romantic flavor. Captured by Spanish forces, he was executed on the field of battle. A strange combination is found in some of his poetry, in which side by side are found amatory and convivial poems in the style of Juan Meléndez Valdés (1754–1817), a Spanish Neoclassic poet whose early poetry formed a transition between Neoclassicism and Romanticism, and also poems with the indigenous sadness of his versions of the *yaraví*, a plaintive Inca song.

Some of the same pre-Romantic tendencies are found in the prose works of Manuel Lorenzo Vidaurre, born in the last decade of the eighteenth century. Written in 1820 and published in Philadelphia in 1825, his *Political and Moral American Letters* contain confessions of love a la Rousseau, political and social ideas, and examples of unbridled fantasy.

Pablo de Olavide (1725–1804) spent his youth in Peru and then took up residence in Spain and France. While there he was known for the notoriously wild life he led, including revolutionary activities in France. At first a staunch supporter of encyclopedist ideas, he later repented of his anticlerical attitudes and wrote poetry in which he sought solace in the bosom of the Church and repudiated his revolutionary thoughts and activities.

One of the truly great literary figures of the period was Felipe Pardo y Aliaga (1806–1868), a native of Lima who was essentially a conservative, but who displayed some Romantic tendencies in his works. Employing an aristocratic tone, he lashed out at liberal writers and ideas as he castigated the bumbling attempts to set up a democratic government. He was the first to write what later came to be called the *criollo* drama, characterized by emphasis on Peruvian customs and language and much moralizing satire. A very correct and disciplined writer, little of Romanticism can be seen in his works. However, he did translate one of Victor Hugo's poems and shows some Romantic tendencies in two poems: "La lámpara" [The Lamp] and "La despedida" [The Farewell]. In the latter the influence of Meléndez Valdés is evident as Pardo demonstrates a Romantic uneasiness.

Another dramatist who composed *criollo* plays during the same period was Manuel Ascencio Segura (1805–1871). An army man who fought against Sucre at Ayacucho and later filled political positions, he wrote satirical plays which are similar to Pardo's drama, except that the moralizing note is absent and the author is careless in form and style. Possessed of a very perceptive nature he wrote dramas in which he portrayed the language of the people of all parts of Peru. While Pardo maintained an aristocratic posture as he scored Peru's weaknesses, Segura identified himself with the people. He created human beings and sparkling dialogue, even though his characters were actually, more than anything else, social types. Thus he helped create a national literature because he loved his country and could laugh at himself and his native land in a laughter that scoffed but was understanding.

Until the year 1842, Neoclassicism continued to be the dominant influence, although the sparks of Romanticism were glowing brighter and brighter. In that year there arrived in Lima the first of the champions of the new literary movement, a Spaniard by the name of Sebastián Lorente. Lorente, a young and fiery professor, was named rector of the Colegio de Nuestra Señora, which was to become the training ground for many of Peru's most brilliant and successful young men. This position afforded Lorente an ideal opportunity for helping to sweep away the colonial Classicism which had kept Peru in bondage for many decades. The most vigorous of these firebrands, however, was another Spaniard, Fernando Velarde, a man of marked sensuality and boldness who had lived in Cuba many years before arriving in Lima in 1847. He was received with open arms by the local poets and had barely set foot in the capital city when he published *Flores del desierto* [Flowers of the Desert], a collection of poetry containing a prologue by Alcalá Galiano. In reality, this volume was a battle cry in which Velarde proclaimed the superiority of artistic freedom to what he considered the straitjacket of Neoclassicism. A very egotistical young man of just twenty-four years of age, he struck out right and left wounding susceptibilities as he excoriated all writers whose works betrayed the slightest evidence of Neoclassicism, including Felipe Pardo y Aliaga. In spite of the fact that he made some enemies, the young Peruvian writers took him to their bosoms and praised his talent and his fighting role in almost hyperbolic language. But although Velarde became the hero of most of the rising generation of men of letters, he found it difficult to accept criticism, an attitude which caused him much unhappiness. When his volume of poetry was criticized, he became irate and left Peru. Later he wrote a poem in which he severely lashed the Lima which had welcomed him so generously when he was still just a young man. Many years later he repented of his petulant action and attributed it to personal pique.

The role foreigners played in bringing new ideas into Peru is emphasized by Luis Alberto Sánchez, who wrote: "Between the years of 1844 and 1864, there developed in Peru a phenomenon of transculturalization, of direct assimilation from foreign schools and tendencies, one which had never been seen before, not even during the days of the wars for independence."[1]

It is revealing to note that Lorente and Velarde were not the only foreign visitors who fanned the flames of Romanticism. Among the others were Domingo Faustino Sarmiento, the great Argentine writer and politician; Francisco Balboa, a Chilean writer exiled for his liberal publications and activities; his brother Manuel; and Benjamín Vicuña Mackenna, another Chilean who felt the wrath of Chilean President Echenique. All of these Chileans wrote works dealing with Peru. Francisco Balboa wrote a work treating Santa Rosa de Lima; his brother wrote about one of Peru's most popular caudillos, General Felipe Santiago Salaverry, and the Inquisition in Peru; and Mackenna published a history of the struggle for independence in Peru.

The first Peruvian novel, *El Padre Horán* [Father Horán], written by Narcisco Aréstegui, was published in 1848 and although the author did not belong to the generation of Romantic writers, the novel revealed some Romantic tendencies. In a plot where emotions are allowed to go unchecked and romantic liberal thoughts are evident, a friar who is a confessor murders a penitent Catholic. This plot was based on an event which took place in Cuzco.

Thus it was that the stage was set for Ricardo Palma and his fellow writers in a period the great traditionist later characterized as "The Bohemia of My Times." It lasted from 1848 to 1860 and saw the development of many significant Peruvian writers, young men who were in love with the writings of the great Romantic writers of their day. Under the leadership of Velarde they penned dramas and poetry which gave them a certain recognition. But in spite of the expression coined by Palma, they were not really bohemians. Artistic rebels and political liberals, yes, but not bohemians. They were not poor and they did not suffer. They had jobs which afforded them a good living and made it possible for them to publish their works without real hardship. However, they were good friends, shared the same literary ideals, and reveled in the intoxication of the moment. These associations were of great importance in the development of the greatest of them all— Ricardo Palma, traditionist.

One of the most interesting aspects of Palma's career is the role that Romanticism played in his writings. As we have seen he grew up in a period when Romanticism was the passion of the times for young writers. Neoclassicism had been swept aside by zealous literary rebels for whom Romanticism was the newly revealed gospel. This was an exciting time for Palma and his friends. The driving out of Peru's Spanish rulers had caused a feeling of great expectations as Peruvians looked to a future of freedom, independence, and responsible government. When political turmoil shattered these hopes, disillusionment set in. And when Castilla became president and perpetuated himself in office for almost twenty years, political idealists—or should we call them liberals or Romantics?—chafed under his rule and opposed him, especially in the columns of newspapers. Romanticism, therefore, was in the air in politics and literature, and Palma breathed deeply of it.

How Romanticism developed in Palma is not well delineated. We know about his friends who were Romantics and we know something about the influence of writers like Julio Arboleda, a Colombian who motivated Palma to write about New World themes. Another foreigner who influenced Palma was the Argentine Juana Manuela Gorriti, whose interest in native themes possibly spurred Palma on to write about the Incas. We also know which Romantic writers Palma and his friends enjoyed. But the study of Palma's early Romanticism is not an easy task. To do this we must study his poetry, his drama and his newspaper contributions because he wrote few "tradiciones" during the early portions of his career. However, not all of his early poetry has been collected, all but one of his dramas he destroyed and almost all of his newspaper contributions either lie untouched in Peru's libraries or have long since disappeared. Add to this the fact that Palma's private library was put to the torch by Chilean soldiers during the War of the Pacific in 1881 and it is easy to see why the investigation of the early years of Palma's career is beset with difficulties. I have collected some of his early poetry which was scattered through periodicals and I have studied poems which Palma published in book form. These sources have proved invaluable in showing very clearly that at first his Romanticism was very strong, then became weaker and finally disappeared, at least in its more apparent outward aspects.

Some of his earliest "tradiciones" show an interest in Indian themes but narratives dealing with Inca times soon lost their appeal for him. An example of this type of "tradición" is "La muerte en un beso" [Death in a Kiss], first written in 1852 under a different title. A Romantic piece of a different type is "Infernum el Hechicero" [Infernum the Sorcerer], written in 1854. Never included in any collection, it demonstrates the appeal that the dashing Felipe Santiago de Salaverry had for him. Salaverry had revolted against President Orbegoso and after defeating him had proclaimed himself Commander in Chief of Peru in 1835. He was young, imaginative, idealistic, and possessed a keen mind. He caught the fancy of thousands and became a popular hero. Captured by Santa Cruz, he was executed in Arequipa and thus became a kind of martyr. Later on, when Palma had rejected Romanticism almost completely, he still wrote about Salaverry in his "tradiciones" but emphasized his ability to grasp situations, his heroism, and his love of country instead of his tragic death.

Just what motivated Palma to begin to play down the Romanticism in his writings is not clear. Perhaps the fact that he was older and more mature had something to do with it. Perhaps his role in an abortive attempt on Castilla's life, which brought about his exile to Chile, sobered him and helped to shake him out of his Romantic daydreams. And perhaps the trend toward other literary tendencies such as Realism and Naturalism was significant. Whatever the cause might have been, in 1860 his "tradición" entitled "Un bofetón a tiempo" [A Slap in Time] contains a sentence which indicates that his attitude toward Romanticism was changing, that what had been almost a religion with him could now be treated in a whimsical way. This sentence reads: "It was our good fortune, or our bad fortune, to be born in this century of coal so enthralled by the Romanticism of Victor Hugo, little interested as I am in the literary style of the days of Calderón." Another piece, "La casa de Pilatos" [Pilate's House], published a few years later, shows us that Palma is now making fun of Romanticism as he describes a secret passage and all of the Romantic characters and paraphernalia that some writers might enjoy putting in them.

In 1872 Palma watched in horror as a close friend, President Balta, was assassinated. This event probably helped to loosen even more the bonds that tied him to Romanticism. In the "tradiciones" and in his poetry written during the next several years we see that the more obvious characteristics of Romanticism have disappeared. But that bloody year may have also accomplished the opposite effect. As he tried to escape from the present, the Romantic tendency to find inspiration in the past was strengthened. Peru's history, especially her colonial history, provided him with the broad canvas on which he would paint his individualized perception of an epoch which fascinated him and offered the raw materials for a whimsical portrayal of the past. Thus his very deep Romantic bent was reinforced but his style and his plots became more realistic as the years went by.

Childhood

Ricardo Palma, whose given name was really Manuel, was born the seventh day of February, 1833, in Lima, Peru, the son of Pedro Palma. His father was a merchant who was living at the time on Puno Street, next to the central market of Lima and close to the square known as Plaza Bolívar, which had been previously called the Plaza de la Inquisición. The location of Palma's birthplace is very important because from the very first, his life was destined to touch both the past and the present of Peru. In the Plaza de la Inquisición he became acquainted with the cells of the dreaded Holy Office, which were used as late as 1820. Other buildings within a short distance from the house on Puno Street were the University of San Marcos, the government palace, the main cathedral, the archbishop's palace, and the church of San Francisco. Although his greatest success was to rest on his literary treatment of the past, he was fated to play a part in some of the political upheavals which wracked his country during the nineteenth century.

For many years Ricardo's mother was assumed to be Guillerma Carrillo Pardos because Palma's baptismal certificate so states. However, his marriage certificate reads, in part: "D. Ricardo Palma, bachelor, inhabitant of Lima, forty-three years old, the legitimate child of Don Pedro Palma and Doña Dominga Soriano." According to investigations by Raúl Porras Barrenechea, Guillerma Carrillo Pardos was actually Palma's grandmother.[2] His mother, whoever she was, disappeared from Palma's life while he was still in his infancy and research has failed to shed any light on her identity. Palma himself never mentioned her, for what reason we can only speculate. Perhaps he never really knew her and perhaps the birth was illegitimate, or at least clouded by some irregularity. Whatever the reason, the matter of her identity has become an impenetrable mystery, one of many associated with the life of Ricardo Palma.

Little is known of Palma's very early years except that he was raised by his father and his grandmother and that when he was six years old his family moved to Rastro Street. While he was living there an incident took place which Palma later incorporated into the "tradición" called "Una visita al mariscal Santa Cruz" [A Visit to Marshal Santa Cruz], which is the last "tradición" he published. In it we are told that one night in January, 1839 the young boy heard hoofbeats on the streets near his home, and, running to the balcony, he shouted: "¡Viva Santa Cruz!" His father was a staunch supporter of Marshal Santa Cruz (who wanted to establish a Peruvian-Bolivian confederation), and young Ricardo must have heard many political discussions in his home in which the name Santa Cruz was mentioned. The marshal had become one of Palma's boyhood heroes, and the child's shout was intended to cheer the forces fighting under Santa Cruz. (Palma did not know it at the time, but one of the shadowy riders passing down the street near his home was the marshal himself. He had been defeated at Yungay [while attempting to effect the union of Peru and Bolivia] and was fleeing the country.) When Palma met Santa Cruz years later in France, the marshal recalled with a great deal of interest the incident in which his guest had played the leading role. The shout startled Santa Cruz because he had ridden directly to Lima from the scene of his defeat and felt sure that the news of the debacle had not reached that city. Furthermore, he was certain that no one knew that he was in Lima. His first reaction when he heard the shout was to change his plans and retire from Lima instead of spending the night there. However, after thinking the situation through, he continued on his way to the home of a friend in Lima. Thus, at a very early age, Ricardo Palma, without knowing it, had seen a great Peruvian of his day and had played an important role in an episode which would one day become a "tradición."

School Years

It is difficult to say at what age Ricardo began to listen to the delightful stories told by a mysterious personage referred to as "tía Catita." In Raúl Porras Barrenechea's opinion, one of the greatest influences on Palma's life was exerted by this woman.[3] Palma himself, in the "tradición" entitled "¡Ahí viene el cuco!" [Here Comes the Bogeyman] mentions her, saying: "That blessed old woman. . .for some youngsters was 'my Aunt Catita' and for others 'my one-eyed grandmother. . . .' " In this "tradición" she is pictured gathering together the children of the neighborhood on moonlit nights to charm them with her stories of witches, of souls in torment, and of the days of yore in Lima. This fascinating person told her stories in the salty, piquant language for which Lima is famous, if we accept as authentic the word pictures drawn of her by Palma in the "tradiciones" entitled "La misa negra" [Black Mass] and "Traslado a Judas" [A Summons for Judas]. It is probable that in the hours during which the boy listened to her, with ears tingling and his imagination fired, something was touched which would motivate him to write of the Lima that was so dear to Catita's heart. From these pleasant interludes Palma gained a devotion for the shadowy events of the past and a firsthand knowledge of the way to tell a story in the popular language of Lima. Palma attended three schools before he enrolled in the Convictorio de San Carlos, the school that he writes about in *The Bohemia of My Times*, which is a collection of reminiscences about friends of his youth. He may have been an able student, but he was too restless and mischievous to spend all of his time in school. He was a freedom-loving boy who spent many hours playing hooky and taking part in such activities as climbing over walls, romping in gardens, watching cock fights, enjoying puppet shows, and relaxing in beautiful spots such as the wooded area next to the pool of the Santa Beatriz estate.

At times his activities were less idyllic, as when he and his friends would visit the place where criminals were executed, just to look at the bodies left swaying at the ends of ropes. On other occasions he threw rocks at nettled citizens and harried policemen, escaping just in time from the wrath of these indignant people. Through all this he acquired a love and devotion for Lima that would make him an able interpreter of the spirit of the City of Kings, as Lima is sometimes called.

The Convictorio de San Carlos, which was under the direction of Don Bartolomé Herrera, a man of unquestioned character, rigid discipline, and intellectual prowess, was a center of intense activity which, says César Miró, was known in all parts of the continent for its educational achievements.[4] Palma was not successful in his studies at the Convictorio, in spite of his intellectual endowments. It was considered quite an honor to be admitted into this institution, which was very dear to the president of Peru, Ramón Castilla. Nevertheless, Palma preferred writing verses to studying the classics and associated himself with the Romantic young liberals of that epoch. His friends included some of the outstanding Peruvian writers of the nineteenth century—Arnaldo Márquez, Clemente Althaus, Luis Cisneros, Augusto Salaverry, Pedro Paz Soldán, and others whom he lists in *The Bohemia of My Times*. The entire group detested "everything that smelled of Classicism" and surfeited themselves on the works of the French poet and novelist Victor Hugo, the poetry of Lord George Gordon Byron, the great English writer, and the works of many

Spanish writers, including José Zorrilla, poet and dramatist, Mariano José Larra, novelist and essayist, and José Espronceda, poet and novelist. The greatest achievement possible for these young men was to write Romantic verses which the public would applaud. Palma wrote his share of the sentimental lachrymose, and grandiloquent poetry then in style, but later in life he turned his back on it, considering such effusions of little value.

Earliest Works

On August 31, 1848, when but fifteen years old, he published his first verses in the newspaper *El Comercio*. They were written in memory of Petronila Romero, a woman about whom nothing is known. These verses were followed by others in November of the same year, written in memory of President Gamarra. Thus Palma, who now signed himself Manuel Ricardo Palma, made his entry into the world of letters. Another genre which made a great impression on Palma during these early years was the drama. The year of Palma's birth came three years after the first presentation of Victor Hugo's *Hernani,* the dramatic event which, although strongly opposed by the Neoclassicists, established Romantic drama on the French stage.

In Peru his fellow bohemians Nicolás Corpancho and Arnaldo Márquez successfully staged patriotic and exotic plays which awakened in Palma the desire to demonstrate his abilities as a playwright. At the age of seventeen he wrote his first work, *La hermana del verdugo* [The Executioner's Sister], whose plot he later incorporated into a "tradición" under the name "El verdugo real del Cuzco" [The Royal Executioner of Cuzco]. Palma himself referred to it in *The Bohemia of My Times* as a "hair-raising abomination in four acts." Despite his later contempt for the work, the verses were applauded enthusiastically by the public. The plot, although extravagant, shows Palma's historical bent, for the germ of the story is found in the executions which took place after Gonzalo Pizarro was defeated by royalist forces at Sacsahuamán in 1565. His second drama, *La muerte o la libertad* [Death or Liberty], a patriotically truculent work, was also received enthusiastically, although Palma thought, years later, that the audience should have thrown their chairs at him instead of applauding and cheering.

Rodil, his most successful play, was first given on January 13, 1852. Received warmly because it contained certain verses of political criticism, the work caused Palma to write later, perhaps somewhat in jest, that at the time of his triumph he considered himself a great dramatist whose success even Victor Hugo would have envied. However, it too was to be castigated by its creator, who said of it years later: "That wasn't a drama or anything of the kind. Coarse poetry, silly lyricism, extravagant dialogue, improbable plot, incidents dragged in for the sake of convenience, impossible characters . . . well, that was a monstrous creation that deserved a sound thrashing."[5]

Apprenticeship

Palma's literary contributions appeared not only in *El Comercio,* but in rabidly liberal newspapers such as *El Heraldo de Lima* [The Lima Herald], *El Correo del Perú* [The Peru Courier], *El Diablo* [The Devil], *El Zurriago* [The Whip], *La Campana* [The Bell], *El Talismán* [The Talisman], and *La Broma* [The Joke]. He also contributed pieces to *La Ilustración* [The Illustration], a magazine. Many of his contributions were political in nature and are of little importance nowadays, but some of them are significant in his development as a writer.

His first literary prose is "Consolación," a Romantic memoir of unrequited love which he penned in 1851. In spite of its sentimental nature, it was based on fact, a "reminiscencia fiel," says Palma.[6] The second narration in prose which he wrote is "La muerte en un beso" [Death in a Kiss], written in 1852 while he was still a student in the Convictorio. Palma refused to call it a "tradición" when he included it in his last collection of *Tradiciones;* he preferred to call it a short Romantic novel. Inspired by "Gonzalo de Oyón," an epic poem by the Colombian Julio Arboleda, this story, states Palma, was well received by the press[7] and pointed the direction in which his talents would lie. His prose, though Romantic in style, showed promise, and his plot, also Romantic, demonstrated his ability to delineate situations and characters with concision and with telling effect.

With these two pieces Palma started along the path which would lead him to the invention of a type of prose expression that would give him lasting fame. It has been said that Palma invented a new genre when he hit upon the "tradiciones." (There is no English equivalent for this term, and therefore "tradición" will be left untranslated.) Certainly it did not spring from a vacuum; it bore a resemblance to many literary types such as short stories and *cuadros de costumbres* (prose fiction stressing the portrayal of manners, customs, and characters of a particular social or provincial milieu), legends, historical novels, and short novels. It is very likely, therefore, that writers of *cuadros de costumbres* such as Larra, Mesonero Romanos, and Estébanez Calderón influenced Palma. The influence of the legends in verse form of José Zorrilla and José Espronceda on the "tradición" is apparent, and the historical novels of Sir Walter Scott and others probably played an important role in the development of the "tradición." However, these pieces are not short stories, *cuadros de costumbres,* legends, or historical novels. In fact it is impossible to provide a satisfactory definition of the "tradiciones" because they are so varied in form, topic, theme, and even in style. Some of the principal characteristics, however, are: (1) they deal with Peru's history from before the Conquest to the period in which Palma lived; (2) they are a combination of truth and fiction; (3) virtually every social type is depicted and the topics treated are countless; (4) the style is generally light, humorous, ironic, flowing, and polished; and (5) because of the ingenious manner in which Palma brings together history, imagination, and an inimitable style, his "tradiciones" reveal the spirit, the preoccupations, and the deepest motivations of the Peruvian people.

Other works of this period of initiation into the world of letters embrace his first romantic legends in verse—"El esqueleto" [The Skeleton] and "Flor de los cielos" [Flower of the Heavens]. These legends demonstrate further a tendency toward the recreation of the past and a seeking for inspiration in the New World. They also show the influence of Julio Arboleda who, according to Umphrey and García Prada, advised Palma to find his inspiration in the history of America, rather than in European literature.[8]

Palma and his associates of the bohemian life found fast friends in Juana Manuela Gorriti and Don Miguel de Carpio, in whose homes the young Romantic writers encountered kindness and hospitality. Juana Manuela Gorriti had written a novel entitled *La quena,* which according to Palma was, after Jorge Isaac's *María,* the most beautiful novel written in Latin America.[9] Don Miguel, magistrate and man of letters, invited the young men to a nightly *tertulia* and regaled them with food and discussions of the arts. He also became their protector, making money available to them and exerting his influence in their behalf.

Don Miguel held a very special place in Palma's heart because of a certain kind act he performed for the student. Realizing that some of the youths could not count on financial support from their families, Carpio obtained for several of them a position in the navy which paid thirty-two pesos a month and authorized the wearing of a handsome navy uniform. Since they were not on active duty, they were allowed to continue their studies while they drew their monthly pay. Little did Palma realize when he accepted the position that the uniform he would wear would be very instrumental in bringing about a radical change in his life. This change would be precipitated by a question of honor.

In 1853, young Ricardo fell in love with a beautiful girl. One day in August he noted that she had been left at home, alone; so he took advantage of the opportunity to slip in to see her. Hardly had the conversation begun between the two when the suspicious mother unexpectedly appeared and found Palma alone with her daughter. Amid threats and accusations, the indignant lady pointed out that her daughter's honor had been compromised. The harried student received an ultimatum from the mother—marriage within twenty-four hours. Palma, just twenty years old and unwilling to give up his status as a bachelor, fled Lima and accepted a position as navy purser on the ship *Libertad.* Although the next verses he wrote proclaimed his love for the girl he left behind, his passion for her died when the notice arrived that she had married another.

Later he transferred to the *Rímac,* the pride of Peru's warships. The vessel's library contained the Rivadeneyra collection of Spanish literature, works which he read avidly during a prolonged stay on the Chincha Islands. Here he found a pure Spanish language in works of sobriety and tested value, shorn of the extravagant plots and weighty verbiage so common at the time. And he found, digested, and later sought to emulate the masters of Castilian humor and irony in prose— Cervantes and Quevedo.

The *Rimac* was important to Palma for other reasons. On a March night in 1855, the proud ship struck some reefs off the Peruvian coast and began to sink. A search for the captain proved to be in vain; he had been one of the first to abandon ship. Palma, on the other hand, carried out his responsibilities and organized the abandoning of the *Rimac*. The survivors landed on a sandy shore and then walked across the desert for three days before they reached a village and water. Twelve men died at sea; sixty-six perished in the desert. This history was to become a part of the "tradición" "Orgullo de cacique" [Pride of a Cacique], which was included in Palma's fifth series of *Tradiciones peruanas*.

Some time before November, 1860, during which month he took part in an uprising against the government, Palma returned to civil life. Attracted to a fiery young liberal, José Gálvez, Palma put his pen at the disposal of his idol, repeatedly attacking the president of Peru and his policies. Words led to actions, the dawn of November 23, 1860, witnessing an attack on President Castilla in which Palma took an indirect part. The attempt failed, as had plans to assassinate Castilla four months earlier, and the instigators of the latest plot found themselves threatened by imprisonment. Gálvez immediately sought refuge in the Chilean embassy and later was exiled to France; Palma, feeling, perhaps, that the battle to unseat Castilla was not over, remained in hiding for three weeks before finally seeking refuge in the home of the Chilean minister. On December 20, 1860, he left Callao aboard the *Florida,* headed for Chile and exile.

Exile and Politics

Prior to his departure, Palma had been given a letter of introduction by the minister to be presented to a young poetess of Valparaíso, Rosario Orrego de Uribe. Through her interest in him, Palma was privileged to join the literary circles of Valparaíso, where he met some of the great Chilean men of letters—Guillermo Blest Gana, Benjamín Vicuña Mackenna, José Victorino Lastarria, Alberto Blest Gana, and others. Palma was welcomed to these gatherings because of his ready wit and his conversational skill. In such a stimulating atmosphere Palma found it easy to devote his time to literary matters. He contributed his works in prose and verse to two publications: the *Revista del Pacífico* [The Pacific Review] and the *Revista de Sud América* [The South American Review]. To the first he contributed some "tradiciones" and some of his poetic works; to the second, essays of literary criticism, historical studies of the Inquisition, more "tradiciones," and some poetry.

Palma had begun to write "tradiciones" before arriving in Chile; however, his output was small and his literary goal uncertain until he began to write his *Anales de la Inquisición de Lima* [Annals of the Inquisition in Lima]. Later he stressed the importance of this work on the *Tradiciones peruanas* when he wrote: "This book [the *Anales*] caused the idea to spring into my head to write 'tradiciones.' "10

The poetry was later collected and published under the name *Armonías* [Harmonies]; the historical studies of the Holy Office were published in 1863 in Peru under the title *Annals of the Inquisition of Lima;* and some of the "tradiciones" were later published with others in the First Series of *Tradiciones,* dated 1872.

This very fruitful period of official exile came to a close in October of the year 1862 when Castilla, true to his promise not to seek reelection, left the governing power to a duly elected opposition leader, who immediately published a law of amnesty for political exiles. Strangely enough, in view of Palma's love for Peru and the rise to power of his idol, José Gálvez, Edith Palma says that the writer of the *Tradiciones* remained in Chile until August 1863.11

When Palma did return to Peru he was immediately named consul to Para, Brazil, a position which afforded him the opportunity of meeting Gonçalves Dias, the Brazilian poet. The two met in Paris when Palma, feeling that the Brazilian climate was injurious to his health, left Para after a short stay.12 Dias, an enthusiastic admirer of Heinrich Heine, insisted that Palma read the works of the German poet. However, the Peruvian did not open any of Heine's collections of poetry until after he had said good-bye to Dias and was on his way back to Peru. In order to relieve the boredom of the voyage, Palma began to read a French translation of Heine's works which Dias had given him, becoming so interested in the verses that for three days he read them constantly and translated some of them into Spanish. Heine became one of Palma's favorite poets and may have exerted a strong influence upon his writings.

In addition to visiting Paris, Palma also traveled to London, Venice, and New York before returning to Peru. He also found time to publish two volumes while in Paris: *Armonías, libro de un desterrado* [Harmonies, Book of an Exile] and *Lira americana* [American Lyre], the latter a collection of poetry of the best poets of Peru, Chile, and Bolivia. From a literary point of view his political appointment had been a success.

Soon after his return in 1865 he was placed in charge of a department of the Ministry of War, which was then being directed by José Gálvez. This close association with Gálvez was to continue until 1866, when the latter fell mortally wounded in the explosion of a powder magazine at Callao during an attack by Spanish naval forces. The bombardment of Callao marked the end of hostilities between Spain and Peru in a war which started in 1864, when the Spaniards seized the Chincha Islands. The war had grown out of a dispute with Spain arising from indemnity claims for injuries to Spanish subjects. Palma himself narrowly missed death at the same time, having been with Gálvez just before the explosion demolished the magazine. His death was averted because in pursuit of his official duties he had left to establish telegraphic contact with Lima.

As soon as the war with Spain ended, another revolution broke out in Peru, a struggle from which Colonel José Balta, whom Palma supported vigorously, emerged as the victor. This turn of events influenced Palma's life greatly because for the next four years he served as private secretary to the new president of Peru, the triumphant Balta. Before leaving political life he was to serve as deputy and senator in the national legislature during the life of Balta's government and as senator shortly thereafter. At first, certain that Peru was headed for a period of peace with a stable government to lead it, Palma worked assiduously in his various positions to build his country. So occupied was he with these activities that he was able to do very little writing, although he had taken pains to keep up with the progress of literature in South America. His political optimism gave way to pessimism in 1871 when he sensed the troubles his country would encounter during the next elections. The pivotal year 1872, with its horror and disillusionment, was fast approaching. Before it ended Palma would have taken a giant stride toward directing all of his attention to Peru's past, thus burying his life in activities that were limited to a scrutiny and a recording of bygone days.

The election of 1872 saw the triumph of Manuel Pardo, who was not to take office until Peru had been shocked by internecine war. Four colonels, brothers who previously had supported Balta, turned against him when he refused to help them keep Pardo out of the presidency. Balta was imprisoned by them, and one of the colonels declared himself the supreme chief of Peru. The news of the usurpation inflamed the Peruvians into revolt against the colonels, who sought to intimidate the country by killing Balta, who was assassinated in his cell on orders of the so-called supreme chief. This brutal act led to an equally savage pursuit of the colonels, which did not end until they were all dead and three of their bodies had been consumed by fire.

After these ugly scenes had taken place, Pardo became president, and the legislature, of which Palma was still senator, went back to work. According to Miró, the death of Balta so disturbed Palma that politics became extremely disagreeable to him, for although he attended all of the sessions of the senate, he did not speak once after Pardo took office.[13] A letter to the publisher of *La Nación* of Argentina includes the following statements: "Scenes in which we have been actors or spectators cannot be treated without emotion. I prefer to live in centuries now departed. In our yesterday there is poetry and our today is prosaic . . . very prosaic."[14]

The First Four Series

The year 1872 also marked the publishing of his First Series of *Tradiciones,* a work which he regarded as an offering of love to his country. The importance which he placed on his writing of *Tradiciones* is seen in the following excerpt from a letter to Juan León Mera: "Just as I am doing, my friend, you are living in the past. To save literary gems and historical events from oblivion is to serve faithfully the cause of America."[15] His First Series of *Tradiciones* was received warmly by both the public and the press, a success which caused Palma to promise to write one "tradición" every two weeks for the newspaper the *Peru*

Courier. He was not able to keep his word, but he did write many "tradiciones" which became part of succeeding series of his works. The Second Series of *Tradiciones* was published in 1874; the Third, in 1875; and the Fourth in 1877. Others of his works which were published before the War of the Pacific included collections of poetry, historical works, and sketches of contemporaries. This was also the period in which Palma discovered and published the poetry of a seventeenth-century Peruvian, Juan del Valle Caviedes, a significant contribution to the literature of Peru and of the New World.

The years between 1872 and 1879 were ones of intense literary activity and included three events of singular importance in the life of Ricardo Palma. In 1876 he married Cristina Román and settled down with his blonde, green-eyed wife in Miraflores, a resort town not far from Lima.

The following year Palma suffered through one of the most painful periods in his life. In 1877 he published a historical study entitled "Monteagudo y Sánchez Carrión" in the collection *Documentos literarios del Perú,* a work which was published by the director of the National Library, Manuel de Odriozola. The purpose of Palma's contribution was to clarify the circumstances surrounding a murder and a poisoning which had taken place in Peru in 1825. Bernardo Monteagudo, an Argentine revolutionary who had come to Peru with San Martín, was found stabbed to death in a street in Lima. Shortly thereafter, Sánchez Carrión, a Peruvian, was poisoned. Palma maintained that Sánchez Carrión was responsible for the assassination of Monteagudo, whereupon Bolívar, his good friend, had had Sánchez Carrión poisoned. From all parts of South America came denunciations of Palma's accusation, from friend as well as foe. Of course, some of the bitterest criticism came from supporters of Bolívar, who considered this publication by Palma to be an attempt to blacken the name of a man Palma disliked. Castigated severely by historians, Palma, shaken and hurt, withdrew from the field of history, thus avoiding being so wounded again.

Still smarting from the lashing he had sustained during the polemic, Palma received in 1878 the welcome announcement that he had been named corresponding member of the Royal Spanish Academy, an honor bestowed on few Peruvians. His prestige now on the rise, Palma laid plans to enhance the image of that body in Peru and do some research on the Peruvianisms which he felt merited inclusion in the dictionary of the Royal Spanish Academy.

War with Chile

A dispute between Chile and Peru over territories rich in guano led to the War of the Pacific, which began in 1879. It was a humiliating and costly war for Peru; for Ricardo Palma and the belles-lettres of America it was a catastrophe. Chilean troops sacked Miraflores in 1881 and burned Palma's private library to the ground; they also destroyed, sold, or sent to Chile the entire collection of the National Library in Lima. The works in Palma's library numbered about 4,000, including the manuscript of his unfinished and only novel, *Los marañones* [The People of the Marañón]. Some 50,000 books and 800 manuscripts belonging to the National Library were claimed by the Chileans as spoils of war. Just five months before the battle of Miraflores, Palma had been named assistant director of the National Library. In both libraries there had been valuable works which could never be replaced, and their loss affected Palma deeply.

Upon returning to Miraflores and seeing the smoking ruins of his home, Palma said to his wife: "We don't have anything; all of my work has disappeared. I will never pick up a pen nor open a book again." Several days went by during which he resolutely refused to read anything, in spite of the entreaties of his wife to return to the literary world in which his life was centered. Finally, when some newspapers and books arrived from Buenos Aires, the temptation to read was too great, and he returned once again to the printed page.

After the books had disappeared from the shelves of the National Library, Palma penned a vigorously indignant protest against the sacking of that institution. Since the style of the document pointed clearly to Palma, he was imprisoned and sentenced to exile by the Chilean military authority of Lima. Fortunately, Palma's reputation as a writer saved him from having to go into exile again, and after several days he was released from prison.

During the Chilean occupation, Palma's writings consisted of contributions to newspapers in Colombia, Cuba, and Buenos Aires— especially the latter. When the war finally ended in 1883, Palma decided to accept an offer from *La Prensa* [The Press] of Buenos Aires to direct a section of that newspaper. His petition to leave the country, however, was opposed by his friend José Antonio de Lavalle, who proposed that the famous author stay in Peru to restore the National Library. Palma's devotion to culture and his country made it impossible for him to refuse the request, even though he knew that he would make no money performing the task. He would become a "bibliotecario mendigo" ("beggar librarian") if necessary, but he would give Peru a library of which she could be proud once again.

His work in the library, where he was elevated from assistant director to director, was truly a labor of love. During the almost thirty years he spent there he was able to replace the majority of the books which had been taken from its shelves and, in addition, he added some 35,000 works to the collection. A great many of them had been sent to the library by individuals, literary groups, and governments at the request of the director. The library, which he referred to as "my daughter," also became his home, for there he lived with his family in some upstairs rooms. His reputation grew so much that distinguished visitors came from all parts of the world just to meet him. In two short years Palma made the library a place where study and research could once again be carried out, one where Palma could once again turn to his labor of resurrecting Peru's past from dusty, worm-eaten pages.

Declining Years

One of the highlights of his life came in 1892 when he was selected as Peru's delegate to Spain on the occasion of the Fourth Centennial of the Discovery of America, held by the International Congress of Americanists. While he was in Spain he met such literary giants as Marcelino Menéndez y Pelayo, Ramón Campoamor, Juan Valera, Benito Pérez Galdós, and Manuel Tamayo y Baus. He also took advantage of his stay to request that several hundred Peruvianisms be included in the dictionary of the Royal Spanish Academy. He was not immediately successful in this endeavor, although years later some of the words he proposed were accepted by the academy. In spite of the belated acceptance of these terms, Palma bitterly attacked the ultraconservative body for its supercilious attitude toward anything from the New World. He noted that only one-third of his words had met with the academy's approval and that some which had been accepted had been changed to fit Spanish ideas of pronunciation and spelling. The fact that the academicians had flown in the face of accepted South American usage irritated Palma greatly and impelled him to wage a vigorous battle against the use of the academy's dictionary in Hispanic America.

As the years went by, he wrote more *Tradiciones*, more poetry, and more historical articles, but his health forced him to limit his work gradually until in 1909 his doctor told him to write nothing more. Two years later his beloved wife, who had helped him raise their five children in an exemplary home, succumbed to cancer. Cristina's death was a terrible blow to Palma; another one, equally terrible, fell in 1912, when his other love, the library, was snatched away by an ungrateful government. For political reasons his son Clemente Palma had been relieved of a position in the library because of some things he had written about the government. When the director (Palma) proposed a successor, the government ignored his proposal and insisted that another man be appointed. Ricardo Palma, wounded in his personal dignity, submitted his resignation, which was not accepted. When his proposal was rejected again, he handed in his resignation for the second time, and for the second time it was refused. Finally, the government, realizing that Palma could not be forced to retreat from his position, revoked the provision under which the director was to select his assistants and accepted Palma's resignation. The new director was Manuel González Prada, a man of considerable talent who severely criticized the way the library had been run while Palma was directing its affairs.

The irascible González Prada was indirectly responsible for some denigrating remarks made about Palma, although, according to Clemente Palma, his father was not aware of them. Upon perusing some of the books in the library the recently installed director came upon some notes written by Palma in the margins of a book authored by the well-known Venezuelan man of letters Rufino Blanco Fombona. Palma had been critical of Blanco Fombona because in a poem treating Andrés Mata, a Venezuelan poet, the former had expressed libelous and scandalous ideas about Mata's private life. Blanco Fombona sought to gain revenge for Palma's notes by casting slurs on the birth and the race of Ricardo Palma in a prologue he wrote for *Páginas libres* [Free Pages], by González Prada. The Venezuelan, in his mordant, sarcastic style, accused Palma of loving Spain more than America and of blackening the name of Bolívar. He referred to Palma as an illegitimate mulatto and fabricated a vicious story about the circumstances of his birth. His father, stated Blanco Fombona, was a lascivious Negro soldier who had accompanied Bolívar to Peru from Colombia and had raped a poor, humble woman of Lima. From that crime of passion was born Ricardo Palma. This explained, according to Blanco Fombona, Palma's hostility toward Bolívar and his troops.[16] Later, says Clemente, Blanco Fombona admitted that he had written such scurrilous things, inventing the greater part of it, just to wound Palma. He expressed his regrets for the insults he had directed against one of the most outstanding Spanish American literary figures.

This period of grief was also one of triumph, for newspapers and individuals alike leveled attacks against the government for such an unjust action, at the same time showering Palma with praise. At a meeting held in May, 1912 to honor Palma, one distinguished speaker after another rose to pay homage to the former director of the library, and wave after wave of applause from the packed house met their remarks. This was, indeed, a glorious night for the grand old man of Peruvian letters. Rarely had any author received such spontaneous proof of the esteem in which he was held.

His dismissal was followed by his return to Miraflores, where he spent the last seven years of his life with his family. He died in 1919, surrounded by his children, relatives, and intimate friends, his mind clear and active until the hour of his death. In his memory the Society of the Friends of Palma erected a bust of him on one of the main streets of Miraflores. Thus from a location which is a short distance from the home he died in his bust will remind everyone that Peru boasts a truly great figure, Ricardo Palma, who, because of his love for his country and for a literature of high quality, left a poetic vision of Peru which would delight readers for many, many years.

Chapter Two
The "tradición"

The "Tradición" at a Glance

This section provides the more significant characteristics of the "tradición." Because of the varied nature of this genre it is virtually impossible to write an all-inclusive definition. However, no description of the "tradición" would be complete without the following characteristics.

The "tradición" is a short narrative mostly in prose, which combines truth and fiction. Its topics and themes are countless; Palma wrote about anything and everything that caught his fancy. Many of them, especially the more popular ones, are novels in miniature (*novelas homeopáticas* in Palma's terminology). Of course, there are many which are merely a collection of ideas, facts, or literary works. Although the "tradición" is not history, anecdote, or short story, it contains elements of all of them. One of the features of these narratives which attract the reader is their ability to reveal the spirit and expression of the multitudes because they are a reflection of reality.

The purpose of the "tradición" was to entertain as well as to teach and its sources are manifold. Palma found the inspiration for many of his pieces in sayings, words, songs, *pasquines* (verses written on walls), proverbs, customs, superstitions, legends, stories, and anecdotes. Other sources include unpublished as well as published materials. The former include manuscripts, court cases, printed programs for specific events, letters, government records, compilations of laws, convent records, Inquisition records, official edicts, municipal ordinances, chronicles, historical works, and literature. Included in the published materials he used are chronicles, historical works, literary works, the Bible, hagiography, linguistic works, travel books, newspapers, and magazines. Of course Palma drew many "tradiciones" from his own experiences and invented some from beginning to end. (Note: the

Aguilar edition of the "tradiciones" contains an excellent section, pp. 1733–49, which lists the sources employed by Palma.)

The majority of these narratives take place in Peru and most of these are set in Lima. A few "tradiciones" are set in other Spanish American countries and even a smaller number take place in European countries such as Spain, France, Italy, and England. They span a period which stretches from A.D. 1180 to the times in which the author lived; however, some are folktales, comments on customs and sayings, and other types of pieces which have no discernible time setting.

The "tradición" tends to be short. In the Aguilar edition the longest is nine pages ("Los caballeros de la capa" [The Gentlemen of the Cape]) and the shortest is one-half page ("Diego Centeno"). The majority cover two to five pages.

A study of the form of the "tradición" reveals that the arrangements are so varied that it is impossible to include all of them here. In an analysis of the form of the first seventy pieces written by Palma at least twenty-one different arrangements were discovered. In the First Series the most common form is the narrative alone, with no introductory sections and no sections which could be classed as digressions, although in the body of the stories Palma sometimes digresses briefly. In the Second Series, the one which deals with viceroys, the form used most often is the narrative type followed by a digression, which is then followed by the end of the narrative. In most cases the digression is a short historical section dealing with the viceroy of the period and his times. Palma often refers to it as the "obligado parrafillo histórico" ("the obligatory short historical paragraph"). Of the seventy pieces analyzed for form, 23 or 33 percent are of this type. The next-highest category, the narrative with no introduction and no digressions, has nine pieces, or 13 percent.

In the majority of cases there is a minimum of complication in the plots of the "tradiciones"; in fact, in many pieces there is no plot, just a collection of notes about a topic. Some of the plots have surprise endings, but most are straightforward. Suspense is achieved and maintained very skillfully and within the context in which the author is working, the "tradiciones" are plausible. It is true that many "tradiciones" lack unity in the strict sense because of the extraneous material and the multiple narratives found in them; however, a certain loose unity is almost always found because the author relates his material in some way to the topic or story treated. Exceptions to the foregoing include "tradiciones" which are composed of two or more unrelated stories. An example of this type is "Dos cuentos populares" [Two Popular Stories].

All types of characters are depicted: vertically, from viceroy to beggar, slave, and convicted murderers and horizontally we have social types of the lowest levels, the middle-class levels, and the aristocratic levels. In addition, almost all of the important vocations are represented in the "tradiciones." Characters are portrayed briefly, with almost a complete lack of psychological development; nevertheless, although almost all characters tend to be types, they are portrayed so intensely, with their human strengths and weaknesses so clearly delineated, that they seem to be real, live people. Palma pays particular attention to the women of Lima with their beauty, verve, and "ability to tempt a bishop." They are depicted as scheming. emotional, and fluent and witty in their speech.

A treatment of Palma's style, even in this brief form, cannot begin to do justice to this extremely important aspect of the "tradiciones." The material which follows merely touches upon some of the more important characteristics of style. The study of diction reveals the following. Palma uses Latinisms, non-Spanish European words, archaisms, neologisms, invented words (e.g., *milagrear* [to perform miracles]), colloquialisms, jargon, slang, popular idioms, proverbs, colorful metaphors, similes and other comparisons, "pure" Castilian, combinations of poetry and prose. In these pieces the author uses the language of the cultured and uncultured alike. Palma's tone is light, humorous, ironic, satirical, skeptical, irreverent, witty, informal, playful, subtle, picaresque, and mischievous.

Other important characteristics of his style include sparkling, lively dialogue, language which is carefully worked and polished, language which flows very quickly and effortlessly, and a tendency on the part of the author to write short, simple sentences. Descriptive passages are few and the ones that are encountered are usually not long or involved. In his early "tradiciones" Palma definitely reflects the influence of Romanticism, which is very apparent in the emphasis he places on

Nature. In his mature years there is a realistic flavor in his "tradiciones" and the portrayal of Nature is almost completely ignored. One other point which should not be overlooked is that Palma writes his pieces as if he were telling a story to someone. At times he speaks directly to the reader and on occasion he interrupts the thread of the story he is relating in order to inject some information or express an opinion he feels might be interesting to the reader.

The "tradición"—An Examination in Depth

To Ricardo Palma belongs the honor of creating a new literary genre—the "tradición"—a work principally in prose, which, although possessing the characteristics of history, the short story, and the anecdote, is none of these. The difficulty of defining the "tradición" is noted by Ventura García Calderón, who writes: "Like all ingenious and volatile things the definition does not fit into an academic pigeonhole. In addition, 'Tradiciones' change in form and character with the capricious whim of the narrator."[1] Although Palma did not answer all of the questions which have arisen concerning the nature of his "tradiciones," he has given us valuable information about the genre as he conceived it. A letter to Pastor S. Obligado, an Argentine friend who, inspired by Palma, wrote "tradiciones" about his own country, contains the following observations:

I have written the story of the humorous friar as a pretext in order to put down in this letter all that I know and think the literary genre baptized the TRADICION is and ought to be. This genre which is of very modern acclimation into Castilian literature is both a romance and not a romance, history and not history.

The form should be light and should be bubbling over with joy. . .with a rapid and more or less humorous narration. . . . A severe style in the "tradición" would be as appropriate as the magnificat during the matins; that is to say it would not be suitable at all.

Fortunate was I indeed, when the idea came to me to sugar-coat pills and give them to people without the scruples of a silly nun. A few, perhaps more than a few lies, and a certain dose of truth, infinitesimal and homeopathic though it may be, a great deal of care and polishing in the language and behold the prescription for writing "Tradiciones."[2]

The prologue that Palma wrote for a work penned by a disciple of his, Clorinda Matto de Turner, provides these ideas:

Essentially, the "tradición" is nothing more than one of the forms that history can take; but without the pitfalls of the latter. It is necessary for history to narrate happenings in a dry fashion, without having recourse to fantasy and to appreciate them with a philosophical-social point of view and with the impartiality of judgment and elevation of purposes that enhance the image of modern historians such as Macaulay, Thierry, and Modesto de Lafuente. The historical work that disfigures, that omits or pays attention solely to facts that are suitable or seem to be suitable; the history that adjusts itself to the spirit of a certain school or a certain political persuasion is not worthy of being called history. Less narrow and less dangerous are the boundaries of the "tradición." Upon it, upon a small base of truth, it is permissible to erect a castle. The traditionist must be a poet and a dreamer. The historian is the man of reason and of prosaic realities.

A light style, rounded phrase, sobriety in the descriptive passages, rapid portrayal of events, presentation of characters and their personalities in one stroke of the pen, simple and animated dialogue, a homeopathic novel, in reality, that is what in my opinion the "Tradición" ought to be.[3]

That Palma took some liberties with history there can be no doubt, but where history ends and Palma's imagination begins is not always easy to ascertain. Juan Valera, the great Spanish critic and novelist of the nineteenth century, wrote in his *Cartas americanas* [American Letters] that although Palma confessed to using some fiction in his *Tradiciones,* he (Valera) could detect it only in the details. The essential elements of the works, he felt, were completely true, so true that no history, regardless of its sober style and rich documentation, could surpass the *Tradiciones* in giving a clear picture of the Peru that once existed.[4]

In spite of the preceding paragraph, it should be kept in mind that such a favorable view of the historicity of Palma's *Tradiciones peruanas* was not universally held. Manuel González Prada referred to the "tradición" as "that monster spawned by the bitter sweet falsifications of history and the microscopic caricature of the novel."[5] As we have seen, Palma did not hide the fact that his "tradiciones" were not history. When writing to Pastor Obligado he said that it was distasteful to him to think that they might be considered in this light.[6] The tripartite division of many of Palma's "tradiciones" makes it apparent that the author felt it necessary to separate history from the events which he embellished. In the first portion he often introduced the principal characters and began to weave the plot; in the second, he left the narration to furnish the reader with the historical background; and in the third, he would return to the narrative, quickly providing the climax and the denouement.

By making use of this arrangement, Palma can bring his inventiveness and creative imagination into full play. He is also able to present in an oblique fashion a brief historical section which enhances the interest of the work. Actually, Palma at one time said that his purpose in writing the "tradiciones" was a patriotic one. By writing them he would induce the public to read a little of the history of Peru; if the "tradición" merely whetted the appetites of his countrymen, they could search for more information in history books.[7]

Palma's works present a rich panorama of life in Peru from the time of the Incas down through the revolutionary period and into the constitutional Peru which Palma knew. Here we see passing before us the proud Inca, the rude conquistador, the haughty viceroy surrounded by the splendor of his colonial court, the inspired leader of the fight for independence, the reckless *caudillo* who brought revolution and chaos to Peru, and the constitutional authorities who worked to bring about stability. Alongside these characters walk priests and rogues, saints and criminals, nobles and laborers, and Lima women of every type—in short, in the *Tradiciones* the whole canvas of Peruvian society is painted in brilliant New World colors with vigorous, deftly applied strokes.

Not all the "tradiciones" center around some historical personage or event. Palma wrote about anything which struck his fancy, whether it was the miracles of a saint, the exploits of souls in torment, the history of bullfighting, heraldry, or the origin of popular expressions. His curiosity was unbounded and his interests were many. His muse was the people and the dusty documents of the past. His writings found their way into a collection of literary odds and ends—the *Tradiciones*—one series of which he baptized *Cachivachería*—literally a heap of broken and worthless objects.

So Palma, who had once said: "For me this picaresque world is poetic, a little in the present and much in the past,"[8] took the truth as he saw it, embellished it, transformed it, and produced a concise miniature which breathes forth life, and is a dusty remnant of the past which has captured a brief instant and preserved it for posterity. The reasons for Palma's literary popularity are many—humor, interesting subject matter, and the ability to outline the preoccupations of an epoch—but the principal reason for his greatness is his style, which will be discussed in the section which follows.

Palma had many imitators, but no one succeeded in writing "tradiciones" like those of Don Ricardo. Five years before Rubén Darío, the "High Priest of Modernism," had stated: "My literature is mine in me," Palma had written to Vicente Barrantes, a Spanish friend, saying: "My style is exclusively mine; a mixture of Americanism and Hispanicism, with the end result being a pure expression and a syntax that is well structured."[9]

Palma's style is continually emphasized by his critics, but no one emphasized it more than the author himself. In a letter to Juan María Gutiérrez in 1875 he wrote: "I believe that the secret of the 'tradición' lies, above all, in the form. It should be narrated the way stories are narrated. The pen ought to glide lightly and it ought to be sparing in the use of details."[10] To Barrantes he wrote: "For me a 'tradición' is not a superficial thing but rather a work of art. I have the patience of a Benedictine monk when it comes to touching up and polishing the sentences I write. It is the form more than the content that has made them so popular."[11]

In the course of explaining the "tradición" as a literary form to Pastor Obligado, Palma recounted an episode which he had read in the works of Father Isla in which a madman shouted as he walked through the streets of Seville: "Anyone who wants to know how to plug a melon should find out from old Anton." When several passersby gathered around the madman and asked him how to plug melons, he answered: "So you want to know, gentlemen, how to plug a melon. Well, you plug a melon (and this he said with professional emphasis) by knowing how to recite the Creed."[12] What is the "Creed" that one must know in order to write "tradiciones"? To explain what it is, Palma evokes those nights when tía Catita would

weave a spell of enchantment over her young listeners by the magic of
her tongue. These youngsters were delighted to listen again and again
to the very same stories, which seemed to be completely true. Catita
was successful as a storyteller because, says Palma, she knew how to
recite the "Creed." Palma explains the "Creed" in the same letter as
follows: "The result of my lucubrations concerning the best way to
popularize the historical happenings was the deep conviction that the
writer ought to place emphasis on the form more than on the facts
themselves, for this is old Anton's Creed."[13]

Palma felt that the people of Peru were like children, boys and girls
who had grown up but were still fascinated by the skillful storyteller
who knew how to recite the "Creed" the way tía Catita did. He
decided to sugar-coat history for them by telling stories, with emphasis
on the word "telling." They would be written narratives in which the
author would take the liberty of speaking to his circle of listeners
whenever he desired, even though it meant digressing from the subject
at hand. Chatty, informal, frivolous, and irreverent, they would be
sprinkled with colloquial expressions, expressions used in Lima, archaic
words and idioms, proverbs, and a salty, earthy humor, at all times
kept within the bounds of good taste.

We do not know what Catita's style was; however, if we place
credence in the "tradiciones" in which Palma evokes her as a teller of
tales, she used much the same style that the "tradicionista" used in
many of his most delightful tales. It is possible that the "tradición"
which endeared Palma to the Spanish-speaking world was not born
until he incorporated some of tía Catita's storytelling manner into his
own historical anecdotes.

Guillermo Feliú Cruz feels that the first literary contributions which
the writer made to the press in Chile reveal him as a possessor of
mature style in the composition of the "tradición."[14] Feliú Cruz singles
out "El virrey de la adivinanza" [The Viceroy of the Riddle] for
special attention and says of this work [first published in Lima in
1860 and then in Valparaíso in 1861): "The language takes on
extraordinary form; the style is characterized by an admirable
purity."[15]

In his earlier "tradiciones" ("Consolación" [Consolation], "La
muerte en un beso" [Death in a Kiss], "Lida," "Mauro Cordato,"

"Palla Huarcuna," and "Mujer y tigre" [Woman and Tiger]) some of the sparkle, the chatty asides, the apt figures of speech, and the irony had begun to appear, but essentially they are works in which the author writes about romantic incidents in dull prose.

"El virrey de la adivinanza" is a series of episodes in which the author, writing as a storyteller tells stories, digresses from the subject of Viceroy Abascal to remark on the principal historical events of his reign and the difference between the banquets of colonial and constitutional periods. Here his tone is personal, his comments on people and events are witty, and his similes apt and somewhat irreverent. Also found here are the maxim, the colloquial expression, and a complete lack of flowery language. This "tradición" occupies a unique place among its sister works, for in it Palma, for the first time, seems to have developed some concept of what the "tradición" was to be. The writer says in one place in it: "The rest of the important events of the Abascal period are connected with the wars for Independence, and they would require a study foreign to the nature of the 'tradiciones.' " This story was first published in 1860, then in 1861, and again in 1872, when it was included in the First Series. However, it was not until 1883 that the quote given above was made a part of the "tradición."

The "tradición" which is entitled "Don Dimas de la Tijereta" is of special importance to Raúl Porras Barrenechea, for in it he sees the author hitting on the style which will mark his works as original. Says Porras Barrenechea: "But the personal and original formula of his art he will find in 1864 upon writing 'Don Dimas de la Tijereta,' in which he frees himself from routine models. He ventures to use the brisk language of proverbs and popular ditties, and with Creole slyness combines in a savory whole the colonial and the republican atmosphere and the candor of the convent chronicle. In it appears, as a principal character, the Devil himself in a duel of trickery and fraud with a scribe of the arcades of Lima."[16]

This "tradición" appears to be the first one in which the author conscientiously makes use of devices employed by storytellers. The subtitle is "An Old Woman's Tale, Which Tells How a Scribe Won a Case from the Devil," and the work begins just like a story with "Once upon a time. . . ." All of the elements noted in "The Viceroy of the Riddle" are here and are used in greater abundance. They are used more tellingly, and are accompanied by delightful discussions about Adam and Eve, scribes, devils, and justice in Hell. One point noted above in the discussion of "The Viceroy of the Riddle" deserves special attention in the work—the clever use of language. In this picaresque type of tale, the plot turns on the fact that Satan thinks that when Dimas agrees to give his *almilla* to the Devil, he is promising his soul to him. The *almilla*, in this case, is not a derogatory expression for the word "soul"; it is a Spanish word for an interior shirt or jacket. This effective use of Spanish gave Palma's "tradiciones" a quality which enhanced his reputation among the defenders of "lo castizo" ("uncorrupted language"), and helped the past to come alive.

However, if one infers from the foregoing that Palma's "tradiciones" show a slavish obedience to the dictionary and the grammar of the Spanish Academy, he is mistaken. The "tradición," says Palma, is the genre which best represents Americanism in literature. Therefore, it should reveal Latin American customs and personalities, and must, if necessary, sacrifice the purity of the Spanish language in order to present the authentic language spoken by the people. Even provincialisms, slang, and rude expressions must not be avoided, for the author's duty is to strive toward naturalness, not flee from it.[17] Barrenechea says that this kind of approach makes it possible for Palma to use "Latin expressions of college students, short sudden prayers of devout women, colorful expressions of picaresque grandmothers, terms stolen from bullfighters or gamblers, the twisted lexicon of scribes and magistrates, and finally, rhymed proverbs and sentences, popular songs or gay couplets."[18]

Palma's style was marked by a delicate irony so skillfully employed that it wounded but slightly, and by a good-humored waggishness. He is liberal, but not rebellious, as he twits the Catholic Church and authoritarianism, and he does not permit his writings to go beyond the limits of good taste and an interested impartiality. This Palma-type humor, embodied in a racy, colloquial prose which is filled with revitalized and archaic expressions and molded by a sure, skillful hand, is perhaps the principal reason why Palma's works were read so eagerly in all parts of the Hispanic world when they first appeared. It also explains why the "tradiciones" have continued to be popular down to the present day.

Many words of praise have been bestowed on Palma's style, but some of the most complimentary come from a French critic of Spanish American literature, Max Daireaux, who wrote: "The writers of youthful America would do well to study Palma's style closely, because no one has possessed that purity, that grace full of slyness, that liveliness, that youthful expression, nor that sobriety, nor that sensitivity which makes him a classic master, something like a Fragonard painting the Perichole."[19]

No Latin American writer of Palma's day has enjoyed the renown of the "tradicionista," nor is there one of his contemporaries whose works have been published in greater quantity, says Feliú Cruz.[20] His style earned for him an enviable reputation which has not dimmed with the passing of the years. With regularity his *Tradiciones peruanas* are still published and still savored by those who desire to travel into the enchanted past that was recaptured by Ricardo Palma.

Chapter Three

The Evolution of the "tradición"

1851–1858—Beginnings

When Palma first began writing prose pieces he apparently had no concept of what would later be the "tradición." "Consolación" [Consolation], his first work (1851), is a Romantic memoir of a young man who committed suicide because the young lady to whom he declared his love made fun of him in the presence of three girl friends. In a note appended to the piece Palma wrote that the episode described had actually happened during his school years. In style it is typically Romantic. Note the following example: "Youth without love is like a fountain without any murmuring. Love is for that part of life what aroma is for the flower, what blue is for the sky. Take that divine fire from youth and you have robbed it of its illusions, you have snatched away its faith and turned its world into an infinite space in which darkness reigns." Another Romantic passage appeared in the version published in the *Revista de Buenos Aires* [Buenos Aires Review] in 1866 but was eliminated from the Aguilar edition. It follows the passage quoted above and reads: "Then if the young man is named Alfredo de Musset, he becomes a skeptic and dies poisoned by alcohol: if his name is Gerardo de Nerval he becomes impious and hangs himself under a harlot's windows" (Volume 11, pp. 263–264). There are six sections in the piece, all of them brief. The first two sections introduce Andrés; the third digresses on the subject of love and then gets the plot started. The last three sections tell of the tragedy of Andrés with no further digressions.

"El hermano de Atahualpa" [Atahualpa's Brother] was written in 1852 according to a footnote Palma added to the "tradición" (Aguilar, p. 27). Published several times, including an appearance in the *Revista de Buenos Aires* in 1864 and another in the First Series of the *Tradiciones* in 1872, it was eliminated by Palma in the *Tradiciones* of 1893 but was later included in *Cachivaches* in 1900.[1] In 1910 the title became "La muerte en un beso" [Death in a Kiss]. The notes of explanation for the 1900 and 1924 and later editions are revealing because they point out the fact that Palma considered the piece to be Romantic and had been tempted to get rid of it. In 1900 he wrote: "This little novel is a modest attempt. I have great affection for it because, having been written in the cloisters of my school, it merited words of encouragement from the press for the author. It was more or less the beginning of my literary life and I would be ungrateful if I should now throw it into the waste basket along with other discarded papers. Why should I deny Romanticism now, the school with which the youth of my time affiliated itself?" (*Cachivaches,* p. 1). In the 1924 and subsequent editions the explanation reads as follows: "More than a 'tradición,' this is a little novel of the Romantic genre which was very much in fashion in my youth. Written in the cloisters of my school it merited words of encouragement from the Press for the beardless author. I have great affection for it because it was more or less the beginning of my literary life and I would be ungrateful if I should now throw it into the waste basket along with other discarded papers" (Aguilar, p. 23). The theme is impossible love between two Indians, Oderay and Toparca. Unfortunately, a Spaniard, Don García, sees Oderay and swears that he will have her for his own. Don García has Toparca jailed and carries Oderay away by force. Suddenly the door of Toparca's cell swings open and Oderay rushes in. Quickly she tells him she has killed Don García with a kiss. Before she kissed him she had applied poison to her lips. When Toparca learns that Oderay must die soon, he kisses her passionately and the two lovers die.

The following passages from the first section of the "tradición" convey the Romantic flavor of Palma's style. (Alaide is the name used for Oderay in the original version.)

Alaide is the most beautiful flower in the garden of the Americas. A white lily perfumed with the breath of seraphs.

Her soul is an Aeolian harp that is caused to vibrate by the sentiments of love and the sounds it emits are as tender as the lament of a lark.

Alaide is fifteen years old and her heart can't help but beat fast when the image of her soul's beloved presents itself.

To be fifteen years old and not love is impossible! At that age love is for the soul what the ray of the spring sun is for the fields.

Her lips are as red as coral and have a violet's aroma. They are an incarnadined line on the velvet of a daisy.

The delicate tints of innocence and modesty color her countenance like the sunset colors the snows of our mountain ranges.

The masses of blond hair which fall in graceful disorder on the ermine of her beautifully shaped back, imitate the threads of gold that the father of the Incas casts through space during a spring morning.

Noteworthy in these paragraphs is the emphasis on nature, emotion, and descriptive details of Alaide. Also evident are Romantic expressions such as "the breath of seraphs," "Her soul is an Aeolian harp," "caused to vibrate by the sentiments of love," and "love is for the soul what the ray of the spring sun is for the fields." In the "tradiciones" Palma wrote in his maturity he doesn't write about nature, avoids emotional scenes or expressions, uses stereotyped descriptions of female characters, and rejects any Romantic expressions or tone. Thus we see that this piece is, in many ways, very different from the "tradiciones" of a later period.

The third "tradición," "Lida," later entitled "Un corsario en el Callao" [A Corsair in Callao] and "Un pirata en el Callao" [A Pirate in Callao], was included in the First Series of 1872 but was later eliminated. This piece was printed for the first time in 1853 in Lima by the *Mensajero* [Messenger] and was called a historical romance by Palma.[2] This early "tradición" tells the story of a young couple whose marital happiness was shattered when the famous pirate Jacob L'Heremite kidnapped the young wife and carried her to his ship. His lover, Leona the Venetian, poisoned him and then hurled herself into the ocean. Lida, the rescued wife, returned to her home, only to realize that her husband could not love her fully because, although it was against her will, she had been with another man. Resigned to her fate, she entered a convent, sacrificing youth and pleasure in order to return peace of mind to the man she loved so much.

The first chapter is entitled "Algo de historia" [A Little History] and gives the historical background of the reign of Viceroy Don Diego Fernández de Córdova, Marquis of Guadalcázar. Thus as early as 1853 we see in Palma's prose pieces the historical section that is so important a part of many of his highly acclaimed "tradiciones."

Although there are some comments by the author about the past and about some of the conditions of his day that he did not like, this section is very similar to the "obligado parrafillo histórico" ("obligatory brief historical paragraph") that is found in the majority of the "tradiciones" of the Second Series. The story proper begins in Chapter Two and continues in Chapter Three. Chapter Four is a long, rambling Romantic digression about Peru. The ensuing chapters narrate the rest of the story of Lida. At the very end of the narrative, Palma informs the reader that on the Isle of San Lorenzo can be found the tombstone which marks the last resting place of Jacob L'Heremite, who died in 1624.

Once again it is necessary to say that there is little in this piece to suggest that the author would one day be known for his whimsical, brilliant style. One passage is somewhat puzzling if we think only of the prose pieces studied to this point. Palma says after the long digression of Chapter Four: "It is now time to return to our narrative. We have strayed from it excessively, letting the pen glide in a dissertation that is too serious when compared with our characteristic frivolity." Judging by this passage, we must assume that there are early fictional pieces of which we know nothing, or that Palma was referring to satirical articles he wrote for newspapers. Certainly the extant early fictional prose pieces cannot be termed frivolous.

Differences between the 1853 edition of the above "tradición" and the revision appearing in the *Revista de Lima* [Lima Review] in 1863 are interesting and significant. First, we note that Palma, in addition to changing the title, has added a subtitle—"Crónica de la época del gobierno del excmo. Señor Marqués de Guadalcázar" ("Chronicle of the Period of Office of His Excellency the Marquis of Guadalcázar"). "Lida" is divided into seven chapters, each of which has a title, two of which have a decided Romantic flavor, "Felicidad conyugal" [Conjugal Felicity] and "El rapto" [The Abduction]. In the revision there are eight divisions. They are not called chapters and the titles have been eliminated.

In "Lida" the protagonist, Lida Ramírez, married Captain Abigaíl González during the first part of June, 1624. Seven days later the captain received orders to report to Callao for duty to fight against the attacks of L'Heremite. The kidnapping subsequently took place one

June night, but we are not told which one. According to this account
the earliest date of the death of the pirate would be June 8. In the
revised version Palma quotes from a historian, José María de Córdova
y Urrutia, who wrote in his *Tres épocas* that L'Heremite died on June
2, 1624. Therefore, in order to make the chronology fit, Palma made
the following changes. First, the date of the marriage is not mentioned
and second González received his orders ten days after the wedding;
the kidnapping then took place the night of June 1. This reordering of
chronology makes it possible for Jacob L'Heremite to die on June 2.

Other interesting changes are the following. The protagonist's name
is Lida Ramírez; in 1863 it is Lida Farfán. In the original the pirate's
ship is the frigate "Reina"; in the revision it is the "Nereida." Leona
the Venetian is the name of Jacob's lover in the original; in the revised
version it is Leoncia. In "Lida" the pirate has ten of his men assist
him in the kidnapping; in the revision the number had increased to
twenty. There are also changes in structure; there is more emphasis on
the historicity of the piece, and the great majority of the original
sentences have been changed. When Palma told Barrantes that he
(Palma) was as patient as a Benedictine monk in the polishing of his
work he was serious. Of the 232 sentences in the original version, he
substantially changed 216.

"Mauro Cordato," also published in 1853, bears the designation
"Romance nacional" and in the body of the piece Palma refers to it as
a romance. One paragraph of the first chapter is particularly revealing.
Palma writes: "And here. . . , it is legitimate for us to answer the
critics of 'Lida,' poor daughter of our moments of idleness, that upon
writing our romances we have not conceded anything to the vanity of
the man of letters, but to the inspiration of man in general and the
man from the New World who anxiously thumbs through the leaves
of a history of his country." At this early date Palma has expressed
himself very explicitly concerning the powerful attraction of history.
He also alludes to the fact that what he has done is to bring about a
literature which is part history and part romance. It is legitimate to
say, therefore, that by the time Palma was just twenty years old, he
had already established some of the essential foundation pieces for his
"tradiciones."

This narrative deals with a murder motivated by jealousy. Mauro

Cordato, a young man who has been in Lima one year, has earned the
reputation of being a Don Juan. The story begins in a café in Lima
named "El Bodegones" on September 8, 1808. The Count of Santella
and a group of young men are speaking in an envious and derogatory
manner about Cordato's success. Their dislike of him has reached a
high point because he has won the love of Pearl, a beautiful actress
who has all the young gentlemen agog. The count, who is not as
agitated as the others, proposes a plan to eliminate Cordato by having
him believe that Pearl is in love with someone else. Knowing Cordato
to be a very jealous person, the count is sure that his rival will do
something imprudent and thereby eliminate himself from the picture.
The count's plan is successful, for Cordato stabs Pearl to death and
then commits suicide by shooting himself. He is buried without the
rites of the Catholic Church on the Alameda near the Paseo de Aguas.

The revised version, "El mejor amigo, un perro" [The Best Friend,
a Dog], printed in 1877, contains some noteworthy changes. Cordato
arrives in 1810 with a dog who goes to the theater with his master
and behaves like a gentleman. One day Cordato sees Pearl walking
with her husband, Niño de Gonces. He falls madly in love with her
and repeatedly tries to gain her attention, but she ignores him. One
morning, while walking his dog, he sees her and tries to press his suit.
She refuses to listen to him, whereupon he becomes angrier and
angrier. Finally, beside himself, he pulls out a dagger and stabs her.
He then shoots himself. Refused Church rites, he is buried on Ramas
Hill. His faithful dog kept vigil at the grave for thirty days, finally
dying because he refused to eat.

Let us review the changes that have taken place. First, there is a
new character in the "tradición," a dog who plays an important role.
Second, the café, the count and the plot to eliminate Cordato have
disappeared completely. Third, the date is 1810, not 1808. Fourth,
Pearl now has a husband and is not in love with Mauro. Fifth, he
wounds Pearl, but does not kill her. Sixth, he was buried on Ramas
Hill, not on the Alameda.

There are two important digressions in the two versions, but they
are not the same. In the original, Palma attempts to portray the Peru
of the first part of the nineteenth century in one digression and in the
other he describes theater life in Lima. The 1877 version portrays

young men of the Peru of the early nineteenth century and contrasts the way they squandered their money with the way their counterparts of the end of the same century held on to theirs. The other digression gives information concerning suicides in Lima.

The style has changed considerably, also. Romantic expressions have been eliminated and the tone has changed from a heavy Romantic one to a much lighter one in which the author is more familiar with the reader. One example provides an idea of the whimsical style of the revision. "The defamers of that period said (I am not saying it, let the truth rest where it may) they said (now don't get me involved and don't call me a story teller, a gossip or a slanderer). . . . So we were saying that the defamers said (and I repeat, let no one get upset with me and take me to task for it) that the reason for this suicide was that Errea had placed a great sum of money which belonged to the brotherhood of 'O' in the keeping of his son-in-law and the latter did not return the money" (Aguilar, p. 861).

"Infernum el hechicero" [Infernum the Sorcerer] is a "tradición" which was written in 1854, according to Julio Díaz Falconí; it is not found in any collection and has not been published in any form since 1902.[3] The copy of the "tradición" that I have was made available to me by Díaz Falconí, who has pioneered the ferreting out of many of Palma's works which have been collecting dust for many years. In view of the fact that in all likelihood "Infernum the Sorcerer" has not been read by many I will treat it in detail. The story begins in Arequipa in February 1836. During this period Bolivian troops led by Andrés de Santa Cruz were fighting in Peru and had defeated the Peruvian forces of Felipe Santiago de Salaverry, a very popular young leader who had revolted against Luis José Orbegoso and had proclaimed himself Commander in Chief of Peru in January of the year 1835. As the action begins a throng of people crowd around nine bloody platforms where Salaverry and his cohorts had been executed by a firing squad. Palma then digresses, praising Salaverry and speculating on what would have happened if the martyr had defeated Santa Cruz. This is how Palma was expressing himself in 1854:

Salaverry and his noble companions had just been shot to death. With them, perhaps, succumbed everything that was great in the youth of the half century just concluded, because they had never bowed down to the statue of egoism.

They fought for liberty, for the future of the Republic and fate was unjust to them.

With the triumph of their cause, how much less blood would have flooded our fields! Brother would not have become angry with his brother, nor would men driven by ambition have been able to raise their thrones above the ashes of liberty.

Salaverry! Martyr of civic virtue!

Who will dare to speak your illustrious name without removing his hat?

A word [name?] suited for poets! Rise up! And when you sing of heroes sing your most fervent anthem to him.

Thus ends Section 1. In Section 2 the bodies are placed in coffins by a man who states as he carries out his task that the people are like a child who hunts for toys. They are equally amused by standing at the foot of a scaffold or by being involved in revelry. While the last of the bodies were being taken care of, a man, the lower part of whose face was covered with his cloak, knelt before one of the platforms, appeared to pray a moment, kissed the blood spattered platform and exclaimed: "My colonel! If you can hear me in the heavens, accept the oath that I am making now to avenge your death." When he rose, bystanders could see the face of Sergeant Laynez, down whose cheek a tear was running. Section 3 introduces the reader to Doña Clara Armandoz, whose beauty attracted many handsome young men. Present at the bloody spectacle just portrayed she was pale and somber and seemed to be suffering a great deal. Seemingly indifferent to everything, she suddenly gave a sharp cry and fell in a faint. She had heard a voice, perhaps that of her conscience, which said: "You infamous informer, I hope you are damned to Hell!!!" When those nearby went to her assistance Sergeant Laynez was holding her in his arms. "There is no need to be alarmed," he said to them. "Didn't you know that the lady suffers from attacks of nerves . . . of conscience?"

Three years have passed when Section 4 begins. Doña Clara now lives in Lima, where her beauty captivates all of the men of the city. However, she ignores all of them. She loves only her child, a daughter born of a love affair, whose health had been undermined and was now suffering the effects of a cruel illness that relentlessly saps her strength.

Her mother spends hours keeping vigil over her bed at night, bathing her daughter's forehead with her tears. Anyone seeing her would consider her a model mother. One night the child dies and the body disappears without a trace. Section 5 takes place on the following day. A veiled woman knocks at the door of a small house and a man wearing a tunic made of blue wool opens the door and ushers her into a room decorated with serpents and dissected animals. The woman sits down, raises her veil, and says that she has come in response to a letter she had received from him indicating that he would tell her who had taken the body of her daughter and what she had to do to recover it. She then asks God to forgive her for putting herself in the hands of a sorcerer. At this point the sorcerer insists that his guest listen to a story, in spite of the fact that she is interested only in the whereabouts of the remains of her daughter, Angelica. He tells her of a young woman eighteen years of age who was living in Arequipa in 1833 who was married to a rich man whom she did not love. In order to be free of him she had someone poison him. Now a widow, she threw herself into a passionate love affair with a man she had been seeing before the poisoning of her husband. From this adulterous liaison a child was born. Unwilling to hear more the woman rose to leave, but the sorcerer told her to sit down, that he was really Sergeant Laynez, who was now the judge presiding at her trial.

Laynez then continued the story, telling how the husband had not died; instead of being poisoned he had merely been drugged. After Salaverry's defeat the colonel (the husband presumed to be dead) appeared at his wife's home and asked that he be given asylum. However, his wife did not recognize him and denounced him to the Bolivian forces, who executed him. At this point Laynez rushes into an adjoining room and returns quickly with a bundle which he throws on Doña Clara's lap. As she looks at the skeleton of Angelica her lips take the form of a horrible smile and she breaks into convulsive laughter. She has gone crazy. Sergeant Laynez has avenged his colonel by rending the only sensitive fiber in that woman's soul. Infernum was never seen again and the imbecillic people thought that he had been dragged, body and soul, to the hottest regions of Hell by his master, the Devil.

Romanticism runs rampant in this "tradición" in which we see bloody scaffolds, a disguise, a sorcerer, hidden identities, a woman who goes crazy when the skeleton of her child is thrown on her lap, an attempted poisoning, a tear running down the cheek of a battle-hardened sergeant, and situations in which we hear a theatrical oath of vengeance and in which the people believe that Infernum has been dragged down to Hell by Satan. Why did Palma refuse to include this piece in any of his collections of "tradiciones"? The author made no comment about it so we are forced to theorize. There are several possibilities, including the following: (1) the plot is poorly constructed; (2) the piece is excessively Romantic; (3) important information is left out (for example, what happened to Clara's husband after she attempted to have him poisoned and why wasn't she able to recognize him when he returned?); and (4) and perhaps the most important, the fact that Santa Cruz is shown in a very poor light in the "tradición"; in fact, his troops are referred to as "hordes" and the caudillo himself drank himself into a stupor in lewd bacchanals so that he would not have to listen to the cries of his victims. Toward the end of his life Palma wrote a "tradición" about Santa Cruz entitled "Una visita al mariscal Santa Cruz" [A Visit with Marshal Santa Cruz]. In it Palma writes that the marshal was a man who possessed the solid qualities of an administrator and statesman; he also said of him that Santa Cruz was firm in his convictions and had an accurate vision of the future of Bolivia and Peru. It appears that after Palma's romantic and fiery youth had given way to more objective views of history he had become convinced that Santa Cruz was worthy of praise, in spite of the fact that it was his order that sent Salaverry, whom Palma admired very much, to his death in front of a firing squad.

1859–1861—The Emerging "tradición"

One of the first "tradiciones" which contain some of the sparkle and the lightness of Palma's mature pieces is "El Nazareno" [The Nazarene], which was printed in 1859 and became the first of his narratives to be included in the definitive edition of the First Series (1893). Palma made it a part of the 1872 edition of the First Series and in that version he called it a "chronicle." This "tradición" is the story of a young man named Diego de Arellano, who led a very scandalous life in Lima. His perverseness reached such a low point that he swore that a certain virtuous young lady would be his within the month. One night he invited some of his disreputable friends to his home. Taking them to his bedroom, he flung open the door and showed them the girl. Chiding them for their faith in virtuous women he told them that he had originally planned to make her his, but now he would give her to anyone who wanted her. Don Diego is the complete opposite of El Nazareno, a member of the confraternity of Nazarenes who went about hooded and lived the charitable life Christ taught. He gave alms to all the beggars, helped businessmen out of debt, gave dowries to orphan girls, and gave comfort to the discouraged and downtrodden. In the final scene Don Diego's funeral services take place. In his will he stipulated that money left from his fortune be given to the beggars and that a note he had written be read from the pulpit. All who attended the service were certain Don Diego's soul was already in Hell, but much to their astonishment they heard the words read by the priest. "Pray for me. I have been the Nazarene."

The structure of this "tradición" is different from the previous pieces. In the latter works there is one principal story which is well unified. There are some digressions, ones in which the author gives a historical background and expounds on his philosophy of life. In "El Nazareno" there is no historical background and there are no philosophical comments. Section 1 tells of the iniquity and the carousing of Don Diego. The rest of the sections deal with El Nazareno. In the last section we learn that these two completely antithetical characters are really the same person. The "tradición" is really a grab bag into which Palma has deposited a number of episodes which are connected only by the protagonist, who is really a sheep in wolf's clothing. A brief résumé of some of the episodes follows. First, Don Diego punishes a poetaster who insulted him in a street ballad. Second, he fights duels with and kills several young men who haled him into court for beating the poet. Third, he lures the virtuous young woman to his home in the episode given above. Fourth, "El Nazareno" helps a businessman who becomes bankrupt. Fifth, he gives money to nuns who could not take their vows because they did not have the necessary dowry. Sixth, he helps a young girl nurse her aged father and mother back to health. Seventh, in a lengthy section Palma recounts the events of September, 1767, when secret orders were delivered to the viceroy instructing him to expel all of the Jesuits then residing in Peru. When those officers responsible for the expulsion arrived at the convent of San Pedro, they found all of the sons of Loyola waiting for them, their bags packed and all preparations for travel taken care of. El Nazareno had warned them, thus giving them time to take care of their affairs before the arrival of the officers. There were two messages aboard the ship that docked in Callao that day. One was for the viceroy; the other, sent by the father superior of the Jesuits in Madrid, was carried by El Nazareno to the Jesuits in Lima. Eighth, the funeral services and the final paradoxical twist are related.

Although many Romantic tendencies remain, as evidenced by the antithesis in the portrayal of Don Diego, the sentimentality of some of the scenes, the melodramatic funeral service, and turning to the past for inspiration, there are definite indications that Palma's style is entering a transitional stage. The tone in the piece is predominantly heavy and serious, but from time to time we glimpse the more whimsical and satirical Palma. Note the description of the protagonist. "Don Diego was a man of graceful and agreeable behavior, as happy as a lark (*alegre como unas castañuelas*), as witty as one of Quevedo's ballads and as wealthy as a usurer of the kind we meet nowadays." Later, when referring to the will by which Don Diego inherited great wealth from his uncle, Palma writes: "And so at the expense of a generous inheritor and his uncle who had passed to a better life in an evil hour, those ravenous leeches that the Dictionary calls executors made hay while the sun was shining."

The next work, *Anales de la Inquisición* [Annals of the Inquisition], first published in 1860, must be evaluated from several points of view. When it first appeared it constituted an important historical contribution. Palma was the first writer to treat the history of the Inquisition of Lima, and although the scholarly work of José Toribio Medina far surpassed Palma's, the *Anales* must be recognized as a first step. Feliú Cruz maintains that at the time it was published it could be considered from a historical point of view as being extremely complete.[4] Some years later Medina discovered a rich collection of documents in Spain which provided the information for his definitive work on the same topic, *Historia del Tribunal del Santo Oficio de la Inquisición de Lima* [History of the Tribunal of the Holy Office of Lima], Santiago, 1887.

One of the disconcerting aspects of the *Anales* is that in many respects it is not traditional history. The tone in many portions is light, whimsical, and irreverent. Feliú Cruz, who says that the reading is most pleasant, writes: "What impresses us most about [Palma's] study is the animated and humorous nature of the style. There blows through these pages a discreet Voltairianism."[5]

From the standpoint of the development of the "tradición" the *Anales* played an extremely important role. As already indicated, Palma felt that the *Anales* caused the idea of the "tradiciones" to spring forth. In the same prologue alluded to in Chapter 2, he wrote that the *Anales* were also "tradiciones." In his return to the past, his interest in Peru, his sprightly style, and his irreverent attitude toward the Church we see many characteristics which are part of his mature "tradiciones."

"La venganza de un ángel" [An Angel's Vengeance] was first published in 1860, according to Díaz Falconí.[6] Like "Infernum the Sorcerer" it has never appeared in any collection. The version that I have was published in the *Revista de Buenos Aires* in 1866.[7] This "tradición" is in the form of a diary written by a soldier, who begins the first entry, dated December 1, 1854, stating that his cousin Magdalena had told him that she loved him. In the remaining portion of this entry he boasts of the fact that he is a libertine and praises men who find their pleasure flitting like butterflies from one love to another. He then writes what he had told Magdalena the day of the entry. "Now you see that I am frank, that I do not wish to play with your heart, for it is that of a child. Williams has been asking for your hand for a long time. Accept the fact, Magdalena, that if you don't find all the enthusiasm . . . of a soul enlivened by the burning rays of the Latin American sun, you will find the frigid but eternal love of an Englishman." In his entry of December 2 the soldier notes that when he told Magdalena he didn't love her he could see a tear glistening in her eye before she ran to her room. Eight days later he writes about Chorrillos in a section in which there is no forward movement in the plot. Chorrillos, a resort and a gambler's paradise, is roundly denounced by the soldier, who blames it for the ruin of many individuals and even entire families. It is a sink of iniquity in which virtuous wives and young women are subjected to filthy language, all in the name of having a good time. In the entry of December 11 we learn that the soldier's honor is at stake. Williams has gambled with him and has won a considerable sum of money, which the writer could not pay; therefore he gave Williams an IOU. The debt is to be paid on the following day and since he has no money and cannot stand the thought of losing his honor he decides to commit suicide by blowing out his brains. No further entry is made until December 21, when we are told that the soldier has been fighting a dangerous fever for ten days. It had begun when, just as he was preparing to shoot himself, Magdalena appeared and handed him a piece of paper—the IOU he had given to Williams. Magdalena had exchanged her promise to marry Williams for the IOU. The soldier had scorned her love for him and she had avenged herself by returning to him his honor. At that point he fell in a faint on a chair with remorse in his heart for not having understood the heart of this angel. In the entry of December 26 we are told that the soldier has received orders to return to his regiment. He has a presentiment that he will not see Magdalena again and asks to be pardoned and forgotten. Thus ends the diary. On January 5 George, for that is the name of the soldier, died in the battle of La Palma. Magdalena is a virtuous and dignified wife, but there are signs of a mortal melancholy written on her face.

This "tradición" adds little to the development of the genre. It is marked by an overdose of Romanticism, including impossible love, highly emotional scenes, melodrama, Romantic verbiage, and a tragic ending. The plot is disjointed, the characters are merely types, and the style lacks humor and sparkle. In most aspects "An Angel's Vengeance" reminds us of the "tradiciones" written before "The Nazarene"; it is just as Romantic and the style is just as heavy as in his earliest pieces. It is easy to understand why this "tradición" was excluded from the collections. The excessive Romanticism or the weak plot could explain why it was left out. It is possible, however, that there was another consideration, the inappropriateness of the comments about Chorrillos. Palma's attack on the resort city is mordant and slashing, and even though the community may have had some of the imperfections noted, the language employed is inordinate, even vicious.

Another "tradicion" which was published in Buenos Aires in 1860 is "La querida del pirata" [The Pirate's Lover],[8] but this piece, unlike its predecessor, was included in the First Series of *Tradiciones*, even though Palma later eliminated it. The story begins off the coast of Peru not far from the city of Pisco. Matilde had fallen in love with a poor young man named Rafael but had been forced to marry Jaime de Cazares, an officer in the Spanish navy. One night the pirate ship *Tirteo* began to sail away from the Peruvian coast. On it were Matilde and Rafael, now a feared pirate. She had persuaded him to give up his life of crime when the Spanish warships attacked. In the ensuing battle, Rafael was mortally wounded. As she held him and covered his pale forehead with kisses, the Spanish marines boarded the *Tirteo*. As Matilde looked at the commanding officer she gasped, "My husband," for it was Jaime. Quickly she seized a candle and fled. Three seconds later a violent explosion destroyed the *Tirteo* and all aboard. In an epilogue Palma says that on a particular occasion he sailed by the coast where the *Tirteo* went down and noticed three crosses on the hill nearby. When he inquired about them, everyone told him a different story. The story he concocted was his romantic explanation of what happened that October night in 1715. One element of the epilogue is especially important. For the first time, at least in any of his extant pieces, he uses the word "tradición" to refer to his work. The last sentence could very well apply to any of his "tradiciones." ". . .Without further comment I bid you goodnight, curious reader, leaving you free to believe or not to believe what truth there may be in the 'tradición' I am relating to you." Several examples of Romantic style suffice. "Matilde is as beautiful as the first thought of love that passes through the soul of a virgin." "Only those hearts that love and suffer are worthy of envy because there is such enchantment and such deep poetry in those melancholy sufferings." "Constant pleasure produces tedium and tedium is almost death. —Matilde loves pain, because it is the vibration of the most harmonious fibers of her being." The weaknesses of his other early pieces are apparent here. The style is somewhat heavy and even preachy at times as Palma philosophizes on the importance of love and its relationship to the Creation. He states:

Love was God's first thought. —Beauty [was] the complement of the creation. It is for that reason that woman was God's smile when he completed his work. . . .

This [relationship between the Creation and love] explains the fact that we all feel an imperious and sublime desire which torments us without ceasing to have our hearts beat as one with that of another person, to live our lives with the life of someone else. Can it be, perhaps, a memory of our celestial origin? Yes! Like God, man's aspiration is to embellish everything with love. —Only that [love] satisfies Heaven's great exile.

There is no evidence of any kind in this "tradición" that Palma was moving toward his mature expression. Perhaps Romanticism still exercised too much control over him, for once again we find the overly sentimental, the weak, improbable plot, characters who are merely Romantic types, and a style replete with Romantic clichés and passages.

Another "tradición" which did not appear in any collection is "Un bofetón a tiempo" [A Slap Delivered in Time], which was published in Buenos Aires and Lima in 1860. It is a brief narrative called a "history of yesteryear that nowadays appears to be a story." Palma also calls it a chronicle. The plot is composed primarily of an episode in which a young girl was slapped by her mother because she was at her window the night of San Juan, 1690, listening to a masked guitarist play her a serenade. After the slap, the mother rebuked her daughter and told the guitarist to leave the premises. At that moment the mask fell from his face and there stood, not a young man of recognized social status, but a barber from down the street. The chronicle goes on to say that the young girl married shortly thereafter; the slap delivered at the right moment had saved her from becoming the sad victim of a seduction. The tone here is light, the dialogue sparkles, and the author is becoming more informal. For the first time he includes some poetry in one of his pieces. The verses found here were probably written by Palma, who states that they were similar to the love songs sung that night of San Juan.

In the first part of the "tradición," in which the principal episode is not even mentioned, the author remarks about the way things have changed. In the old days a mother had complete control of her daughter and would punish her in an autocratic manner. If she sassed her mother, she lost her long hair to the scissors. If she went to sleep

during the Rosary she was shut up in a convent. But nowadays (in
Palma's time), a mother has to exercise extreme caution. No daughter
of marriageable age could be punished physically. The author also
tells about a group called the "young mothers" who liked to think
they were not so different from their beautiful young daughters. Palma
states the following about young mothers: "Do you want to gain the
favor of a young mother? Tell her that she is as charming as her
daughter." And, he counsels, be careful with questions of age. "Don't
mention age in her presence, but if the temptation should come to you
remember that the number thirty is not to be found in a young
mother's calendar."

Making fun of Romanticism, although not rejecting it completely,
he says that in the love stories being written at the time daggers and
poison are always present. He further states that the Romanticism of
his grandparents led to bloodshed when duels took place and that they
had not discovered that the finest arms for combat are bottles of wine
and the best field a table. A unique fate was reserved for "A Slap in
Time," because it was expropriated and became part of another
"tradición" entitled "El cigarrero de Huacho" [The Cigar Vendor of
Huacho]. Written in 1874, this piece contains almost all of Palma's
comments about young mothers, although he has eliminated the
paragraph in which he counsels telling a young mother she is as pretty
as her daughter and avoiding the mention of age in her presence.
However, significant changes have taken place in the story of the girl
who had her face slapped. Now named Eduviges instead of Gabriela,
the young girl is the daughter of a widow whose name is Doña
Angustias Ambulodegui Iturriberrigorrigoicoerrotaberricoechea. In
the original the mother is given no name; in the revision Palma seems
to have made up for the oversight with a great deal to spare! The
scene in which the slap is administered is the same, except for the fact
that when the serenader loses his mask not a barber but a cigar vendor
is revealed. Unlike what happened in the original the slap did not save
her from becoming the victim of a seduction; rather, it had the
opposite effect, for after that night Eduviges exchanged notes with the
vendor and at times slipped out to meet him in secret. One night the
widow found that Eduviges had run away from home and soon
everyone believed that the cigar vendor, the Devil incarnate in their

opinion, had carried her off. The two lovers were never heard from again, but the author assures us that they fled to Trujillo, where one of the vendor's aunts gave them refuge. In this version there is no mention of a chronicle, no attempt to say that the episode actually happened. We are given the impression that all of the events are a part of the folklore of Huacho. Thus we see that Palma changes things around to suit his fancy and has no qualms about presenting fictitious happenings as events that really took place.

If Palma seemed to be moving in the direction of his mature "tradiciones" when he wrote "A Slap in Time," we are at a loss to explain the swing of the pendulum in the other direction in "Palla-Huarcuna." Also published in 1860, it became a part of the First Series of 1872 and has remained there. Palma calls it a "tradición" of the Inca period, but in reality it is very different from what we have come to consider the genuine "tradición." It tells of the tragic death of two young Indians who had been captured by the Incas. Very much in love, they tried to escape because the girl was destined for the harem of the monarch. The young man died defending his sweetheart and she was sentenced to death, a fate she was happy to contemplate because she knew that soon she would be with her lover. In addition to this brief plot, which occupies just twelve lines, Palma includes material of a prophetic nature which points to the arrival of the Spaniards and the decline of the Inca empire. He also tells the reader at the end of the piece that at a certain location in Peru, between Izcuchaca and Huaynanpuquio, there is a rock which resembles an Indian girl. On this spot, to which the Indians gave the name "Palla-Huarcuna," the girl was put to death, and because of their superstitious nature Indians of that region do not pass by that rock at night.

There is no evidence in this "tradición" of the jocular, delightful style for which Palma is famous. The tone is serious and tragic and the mood is Romantic throughout. One specific proof of his Romantic bent is his use of Indian terms, which appear in italics in the piece. Some examples are *haravecs* ("troubador"), *llautu* (tassel which hung from the Inca's crown), and *guairuros* (fruit of a particular tree, used for necklaces). This interest in Americanisms and neologisms would later become one of Palma's obsessions.

The next "tradición" had the good fortune of becoming part of the

Second Series, the first so honored. Originally published in a Lima
magazine, it was entitled "Debellare superbos" [Conquering the
Mighty]. One year later it appeared in a Valparaíso magazine under
the title "Apuntes históricos" [Historical Notes] and in 1872 it was
included in the First Series. Later, in 1883, it was added to the Second
Series. The structure is simple. First there is the introduction, then
come seven short divisions, the first of which tells about Viceroy
Manso de Velasco and the unlucky date on which he arrived in Lima,
Friday, July 13, 1745. The rest of the divisions tell of the various
conflicts that arose between the Viceroy and Archbishop Barroeta and
of the reconciliation that took place after many years of antagonism.
The reader who peruses this "tradición" in the definitive edition that
Palma carefully prepared will think that when the author first wrote it
he had hit upon the basic idea of the "tradición." In the introduction
he points out that tradition is just about dead in the Americas because
the manuscripts and documents of the Inca and colonial past have
almost disappeared. He then writes: ". . .It behooves the younger
generation to do something to make it impossible for tradition to
disappear completely. For this reason I have fixed my attention on it
(tradition) and in order to gain the attention of people in general, I
have thought it useful to adorn all [my] historical narratives with the
trappings of romance." It should be noted that the quotation just cited
was not a part of the "tradición" under discussion until 1872, when it
appeared in a revision of "Debellare superbos" entitled "Un virrey y
un arzobispo" [A Viceroy and an Archbishop]. The style here presents
nothing new. The tone is mostly serious, but there are some passages
which are very light. In these latter passages we can detect the style of
the real traditionist emerging. Here are some examples. In Section
Two we read: "By Jove if those weren't good times for the Church!
The people, as yet uncontaminated by the impiety which according to
many moves forward with gigantic steps, believed with a simple faith
[*la fé del carbonero*]. What would our ancestors say if upon rising
from their graves they were to contemplate the fact that the temporal
power of the Popes is about to disappear? What would their smooth
skulls think if they should see Congresses which, paying no attention
to past excommunications, ignore ecclesiastical privileges?" And from
the same section comes the following: "The old women say that when

the landowner died his body disappeared . . .; and that late at night it would ride up and down the streets of Lima (undoubtedly to get some fresh air) in a carriage enveloped in infernal flames and drawn by four diabolical horses. Even today there are people who believe as firmly in these kinds of nonsense as they do in the constitutionality of certain legislative reform and in the advent of the Anti-Christ which is near at hand. But let us leave the people with their crazy beliefs and put an end to this."

Another "tradición" which became a part of the Second Series is "El virrey de la adivinanza" [The Viceroy of the Riddle]. It appeared for the first time in *La Revista de Lima* in 1860 and carried the subtitle "Apuntes históricos" [Historical Notes]. It appeared in the First Series in 1872 and in 1883 it became a part of the Second Series, where the subtitle was changed to "Crónica de la época del trigésimo octavo virrey del Perú" [Chronicle of the Times of the Thirty-eighth Viceroy of Peru]. The importance of this work has already been discussed in Chapter 2 and some of the characteristics of the style of the piece have been noted. However, there is one additional fact which should be added. In many of the "tradiciones" of Palma's mature period the author begins each piece with a brief, whimsical introduction in which he explains why he is writing the "tradición." "The Viceroy of the Riddle" is the first one in which such an introduction appears. It reads as follows:

Several days ago we were asking a certain elderly friend of ours about the age of a particular matronly lady and the good old man . . . told us after taking some snuff.

"I will satisfy your curiosity, Mr. Chronicler. That lady was born two years before the Viceroy of the Riddle returned to Spain. So you can figure it out."

That response was as satisfactory as our political situation, for I knew as much about said Viceroy as I did about the hour when that greedy Father Adam first sank his teeth into the bitter-sweet apple of Eden.

"And who was that guesser?"

"Man alive! Don't you know? Viceroy Abascal."

But regardless of how much we interrogated the sexagenarian we couldn't find out anything because he was completely in the dark about the riddle. At that point we set out to pick up any information we could by talking to people or reading dusty old documents, a task which finally produced the results which the reader will see if he has the patience to stick with us to the end of this tale.

Little by little Palma happens upon features that he would someday bring together to make up the "tradición." It was a slow, laborious process as he stumbled along trying to fashion for himself a place in the world of letters. Some writers have the good fortune of gaining success in their first effort or of finding their path after they have taken a few steps. Palma was not so fortunate. Many years would pass by before he would have a clear idea with respect to the kind of literature he would best be suited to produce.

Never a part of any series, "La hija del oidor" [The Judge's Daughter] is another work which deserves a better fate. It was published in newspapers in Lima, Buenos Aires, and Valparaíso; then it was abandoned by its creator. The principal plot deals with two philanderers—one a captain in the army and the other a Jesuit priest. The captain, Carlos Perea, needs money and the priest, Father Lutgardo, wants a woman, so they make an agreement. The priest pays the captain five hundred *escudos,* whereupon the latter hands over to Lutgardo a young girl named Milagro, the daughter of Judge Venegas. Perea wanted to marry her in order to inherit the judge's sizable fortune, but when the girl's father refused to permit the marriage, the young officer abducted her. At this point the principal plot breaks off and the author tells about the circumstances surrounding the expulsion of the Jesuits from Spanish America. Then Palma brings the two threads together when he relates what was found in the Convent of San Pedro after the Jesuits had departed. In addition to digging up valuables left by the sons of Loyola, investigators found the body of a woman in a locked room. In her breast was a dagger. Refusing to submit to the evil desires of Lutgardo, she had preferred to become a martyr. The last paragraph provides a good idea of the style and especially the tone of the last part of the piece. In reference to Milagro, Palma exclaimed: "White rose, cut from its stem, just beginning to open its petals to the kisses of a gentle breeze! I once saw the stain left upon the damp, flat stones of the basement enclosure by the blood which dripped from the stab wound in her breast. And as I

thought of how she lost her life I have offered up a prayer for this
unhappy victim of the Jesuit priest."

One of the most impressive characteristics of this "tradición" is the
lively dialogue, a trademark of Palma at his best. Here is part of the
conversation between Perea and Lutgardo:

> "You are in luck, Captain."
>
> "Not as lucky as you, Father Lutgardo. I don't have a red cent to pay the
> bill we have run up."
>
> "By my faith, you are really unhappy. How can you complain that way
> and be so ungrateful? Even though you are broke, women seem to take good
> care of you. For example, there is that Doña Milagro, Judge Venega's
> daughter, whom you have stolen from under her father's nose and shut up in
> your room. Upon my soul, she is as tempting a broad as I've seen."
>
> "How's that? It occurs to me that you are an experienced sampler of
> feminine delights. Tell me, how much will you give me for the young thing?"
>
> "Always pulling my leg, Captain."
>
> "By the nails of Christ, Father, your eyes are really gleaming. She's yours
> for five hundred *escudos*."

Palma calls this piece a "tradición popular" in the subtitle and in
the text calls it a "romance." It was probably ignored by Palma when
he prepared his collections because it was too much like a novel and
too Romantic. There could be other possibilities for its exclusion,
however. He may have preferred not to wound sensibilities, for he
gives the names of the actors of this drama. Or he may have felt that
he was duplicating information about the expulsion of the Jesuits he
had already provided in "El Nazareno." Whatever the reason, this
"tradición" should not be left in oblivion.

"Tragedia de bastidores" [A Tragedy behind the Scenes], later
entitled "Predestinación," was first published in 1861 and became a
part of the First Series. There is little that is significant in this long,
rambling "tradición," but there are several points which become
apparent when we compare the 1872 edition with the definitive one.
First, the date of the action has been changed from 1800 to 1801.
Second, much more information about the theater has been added.
Third, the titles of dramas in which certain actors appeared have been
changed. For example, in the 1872 version O'Loghlin appeared in

Ricardo III and *Don César de Bazán;* in the revision he appeared in
Ricardo III and *Sullivan.* In 1872 Lutgardo Gómez played a role in *El
pastelero de Madrid* [The Piemaker of Madrid]; in the revision he
acted in *Traidor, inconfeso y mártir* [Traitor, Unconfessed and a
Martyr]. In addition, Palma adds some actors and dramas to the
original list. Fourth, in the melodramatic scene in which the jealous
actor Rafael Cebada kills the actress María Moreno, he stabs her
fourteen times in the early edition and only six times in the revision.
Fifth, in the original there is a brief epilogue which has been
eliminated. Palma did well to leave it out because it adds nothing to
the piece, but it does demonstrate his concern for the historicity of his
"tradiciones." This interest can be seen in the following portion of the
epilogue. "Now that the 'tradición' has been completed, the reader of
it asks the *cronista* for permission to speak. Permission is granted. The
reader then asks what proof the author has that the narration is not
pure foolishness. The latter replies that the facts can be historically
verified by many persons who spoke to one of the principal characters
of the tragedy and by referring to documents which treated that
period."

1864–1873—The "tradición" Takes Full Form

The first "tradición" published in 1864, "Don Dimas de la
Tijereta," constitutes a milestone. The plot is very simple. A scribe,
Don Dimas, promises the Devil his *almilla* in return for the love of a
certain young lady. To this Satan agreed, thinking that the scribe held
his own soul in such disdain that he was using the diminutive for it
(*almilla* for *alma,* which means soul). Don Dimas enjoyed the favors
of the young lady, whereupon one of Satan's imps arrived to carry off
the scribe's soul. Much to the surprise of the imp, Don Dimas
undressed and gave him an undergarment called an *almilla.* The scribe
then declared he had honored his part of the bargain. At this point the
imp whisked him off to Hell, where Satan declared that Don Dimas
had indeed fulfilled the terms of the contract and gave orders to have
him returned to his home.

Although the story proceeds at a very leisurely pace, there are few
digressions and there is no historical section dealing with the viceroy
who was reigning at this time. Palma does give his opinion about

women and their culpability in the Garden of Eden episode and in love-making. Yet he does feel that men should bear at least part of the blame. The author also digresses at the end of the "tradición," where he speculates that the scribe eventually committed suicide. Using this supposition as a point of departure, he tells of the suicide of Judas Iscariot and of the return to the earth of his soul. Because it was very cold he took the body of a dead usurer and from that time people have said that usurers have the soul of Judas.

The "tradición" is told the way a story is usually told. Note the subtitle: "Old wives' tale which tells how a scribe won a case from the Devil." The story begins with the same linguistic formula used with fairy stories: "Once upon a time. . ." (*Erase que se era*). In this remarkable piece Palma is at his stylistic best. He is whimsical, jocular, ironical, satirical, and his wit is unsurpassed. He employs proverbs, idioms, colloquialisms, legal jargon, Latinisms, and archaic words. Let us look at some examples of his skill. While portraying Don Dimas, Palma writes: "They said of him that he had more rooms [*cuartos*] than a warehouse [play on words—*cuartos* were also pieces of money], he was as tricky as could be and had heaped up for himself more doubloons as a result of his cheating, lying and unscrupulous mistakes than could be piled into the last galleon that set sail for Cádiz." Later, commenting upon scribes he says:

May God punish me with a bad Easter, the first one that comes along, if in this physical and moral portrayal of Don Dimas I have had any desire to tax the patience of any living member of the respectable body of the "before me" [*ante mí*] and the "I certify" [*certifico*]. And I make this disclaimer . . . not so much to unburden myself of all my offenses, which are not few, nor to satisfy my narrator's conscience, which certainly does need some satisfying, but rather because there are people of substance with whom I don't want to get involved in any way. And that's enough of sketches and circumlocutions and let's get on with it and let the merrymaking continue, for if God wishes, and time and weather allow it and this story pleases, I will supply more stories abundantly without further intervention from the archivist. Get the wheel rolling and give it a kick! (Aguilar, p. 514)

While describing the young lady Dimas desires to possess, the author writes: "He fell head over heels in love with Visitación, a graceful young girl of twenty springs with a figure and an elegance and that certain something that would have tempted even the Father Superior of the Bethlehemites; [she had] a slim and attractive waist of the 'look at me but don't touch' type, lips as red as cherries, teeth like unripe almonds, eyes like morning stars more deadly than swords and clubs in a game of ombre. Believe me when I say this young lady was as beautiful a rosebud as you would ever find."

"La casa de Pilatos" [Pilate's House] is a "tradición" in which Palma provides information about a house in Lima which was called Pilate's house. He gives the history of the building from the time of the Conquest, when it was constructed, to 1635, when it was occupied by some Portuguese who were accused of heresy and burned by the Inquisition. The owner of the house, a Jew by the name of Manuel Bautista Pérez, was called Pilate by the Catholics of Lima; therefore the building was called Pilate's house. There is nothing particularly significant about this piece in style or structure, but one passage is quite revealing. As he had done once before, Palma makes light of Romanticism. While describing an underground passage which connected the house to a Jesuit convent nearby, he writes: "That passage, which can be visited if permission of the owner is sought in advance, is just what future writers of harrowing novels will find exactly to their liking. In that cellar they can have a wonderful time portraying smugglers, conspirators, counterfeit money, gentlemen in chains, abused maidens, and the whole Romantic arsenal of romance."

Noteworthy is the next piece—"Pues bonita soy yo la Castellanos" [Well, I Am a Castellanos and a Beauty]. The title is a saying Palma had heard in Lima and the "tradición" is an explanation of its origin. Many more times in the future he would weave his "tradiciones" around the origin of a saying or popular expression. Palma excels in portraying the women of Lima, and in this narrative he does remarkably well. Depicted here is the conflict between two women, one beautiful and numbered among the most important aristocrats, the other homely, but the mistress of the viceroy. When the mistress, whose name was Perricholi, made an offering of a very expensive coach to one of the local parishes, her rival, Mariquita Castellanos, was beside herself. Not only had Perricholi made a show of giving the coach to the parish but ostentatiously she had ridden in it along the main avenue to humiliate the blue-blooded ladies who looked down on her because she was only a dancer. Declared Mariquita, "I'll take care of that gadabout. My lover didn't learn to steal from his mayordomo the way the Viceroy did. What's his is his and he doesn't have to account to the King for his possessions. The idea! To come to me with her pride and her fantasies, as if I weren't better than she, the wretched little actress! I am a Castellanos and I am a real beauty!"

The story line continues: Mariquita showed up at the celebration of Rosario dressed in very common clothes and accompanied by a female servant who was carrying a small dog in her arms. The collar around the dog's neck was pure gold and in it were encrusted diamonds as large as garbanzos. Everyone commented on the treasure the dog was wearing, but their surprise reached a climax when Mariquita gave the dog and its dazzling collar to one of the hospitals of the city. She thus won the favor of commoners and the nobility, while Perricholi fell in their esteem. Since then the saying "Well, I am a Castellanos and a beauty" has been used in Lima by women proclaiming that no other woman could surpass them in arrogance and luxury.

Although Palma may not have realized it, the "tradición" had been born. From this point on his prose pieces would be variations of what he had already published. There would be zigs and zags, depending on the historical emphasis he wanted to place on a particular topic, and some pieces would be wittier than others, but in "tradiciones" such as "The Viceroy of the Riddle," "Don Dimas de la Tijereta," and "Well, I am a Castellanos and a Beauty" he had stumbled upon the rich vein which would bring him renown.

One further point should be made. The Second Series, with which, Palma maintains, the genuine "tradiciones" begin,[9] is characterized by narratives in which the events portrayed take place during the reign of particular viceroys. Into these pieces the author inserts background information about the viceroys and their reigns. At first, Palma did this on a haphazard basis, introducing the historical material according to his whims. But in "Los polvos de la Condesa" [The Powders of the Countess], the first piece written after the publication of the First Series and which was included in the Second Series, he uses for the first time the unique structure that readers have come to associate with the "tradiciones" in this highly praised series. He begins the story, then tells about the viceroy and his reign in a historical digression, and then returns to the story, which he quickly completes. In the next "tradición" in which he employs this structure, "Las orejas del alcalde" [The Mayor's Ears], he explains the rationale for it. He writes: "Let's pause, friend and reader, and enter the labyrinth of history, for in this series of 'tradiciones' we have imposed upon ourselves the obligation of devoting a few lines to the viceroy with whose government the story is related."

For our purpose we can say that the development of the "tradición" is complete at this point. It took many years from the time of its earliest beginnings to flower into the robust genre which would bring fame and honor to Ricardo Palma and countless hours of enjoyment to great numbers of readers in all parts of the world. It was not easy and at times there were more zigs than zags, but something spurred him on and thus he became one of the literary giants of the Spanish America of the nineteenth century.

Chapter Four

Life in Old Peru as Portrayed in the Tradiciones peruanas

In order fully to appreciate the "tradiciones," the reader should be acquainted with more than the nature and the historical development of these short narratives. Ideally he would read a number of "tradiciones," but because they may not be readily available in translation the flavor of these pieces will be imparted by treating some of the more important themes found in the *Tradiciones peruanas*—honor, the Catholic Church, and others. Hopefully such a treatment will make these miniatures come to life and permit them to be treated as fascinating pieces of literature instead of laboratory specimens whose lot it is to be discussed, dissected, and disposed of.

Honor

Ventura García Calderón, a Peruvian contemporary of Ricardo Palma, stated that honor was the obsession of colonial times.[1] A careful reading of the *Tradiciones peruanas* supports this statement. Indeed, it is difficult to read any "tradición" set before independence without noting some aspect of honor. The spirit of honor permeates these works and is an ever-present source of drama, possible bloodshed, and shamed, ruined lives. Research reveals that approximately 130 of the approximately 530 "tradiciones" contain principal or minor plots in which honor plays an important role; in about 30 percent (158), the honor theme is developed in one of the plots (principal or minor) or it is significant in some other way.[2] They are a rich source of information concerning a concept which is still the subject of investigation.

Honor and Nobility

During the Golden Age honor was thought to be the exclusive patrimony of the nobleman, in whom honor was innate. Golden Age dramas such as *Fuenteovejuna* by Lope de Vega and *El alcalde de Zalamea* [The Mayor of Zalamea] by Calderón de la Barca portray plebeians who carry out vengeance for the sake of honor, but such instances were not common. The question of the plebeian and honor is complicated by the fact that some commoners felt they were men of honor because their ancestors could boast of pure (uncontaminated) Spanish blood and by the fact that some plebeians were noble because their families were from Asturias or from the Basque provinces.

Here are some honor situations in the "tradiciones" in which nobility is pertinent. It is well known that during the Spanish Golden Age a man of honor felt that it was dishonorable to work with one's hands; in fact the honorable vocations available were very few. An example of the *hidalgo* who considered it demeaning to his station to be involved with business affairs is found in "Después de Dios, Quirós" [After God, Quirós]. The noble and wealthy Quirós was irritated when the nephew of a titled gentleman of Castile turned down an offer made to him. The *hidalgo* had asked for aid and Quirós promised to pay him 5,000 pesos if he would take part in a commercial enterprise. Insulted, the arrogant young man said he would not dishonor his nobility by living like a dry-goods clerk behind a store counter. Quirós, turning his back on the *hidalgo*, murmured, "If you are such a gentleman, why are you so poor? And if you are so poor, how can you consider yourself such a gentleman?"

Several of the characters in the "tradiciones" perform work with their hands even though their nobility remains unquestioned. "La primera campana de Lima" [Lima's First Bell] informs us that Don Pedro de Candia, Knight of the Golden Spur, cast the first bell in Lima and none other than Marquis Don Francisco Pizarro, governor of Peru, worked the bellows. Another titled gentleman who performed menial tasks was the nineteenth viceroy of Peru, Don Pedro Antonio de Castro y Andrade, Count of Lemos. In spite of the carping criticism leveled against him by the aristocrats of Peru, the viceroy had on occasion swept the floor and operated the bellows of the organ of the church of the Desamparados. In addition, he played the organ and sang as cantor in solemn mass, other activities which were considered beneath the dignity of a count. Ignoring the barbed comments of the blue bloods, he continued to do just as he pleased. The pieces "El justicia mayor de Layacota" [The Magistrate of Layacota] and "En qué pararon unas fiestas" [The Upshot of Some Fiestas] are the source for this information about the Count of Lemos.

Palma relates many instances in which nobles would vie with each other over whose nobility was superior. Perhaps the most striking incident is found in "Un litigio original" [An Unusual Lawsuit], in which two gentlemen became involved in a traffic problem in Lima. They were riding in their carriages on the same street but in opposite directions when suddenly at the intersection of Lártiga and Lescano the two nobles found themselves facing each other. Each refused to give ground and let the other pass, so they left their coaches in the intersection and appealed the case to the viceroy, who was to decide which of the two nobles possessed the superior nobility. Because both men were his friends, he found himself both unwilling and unable to render a verdict, so he sent the case to Spain for His Majesty's decision. In the meantime the coaches remained in the intersection. Two long years dragged by before the decision was received and by this time both coaches had disappeared; the weather had taken its toll and passersby had taken wheels, doors, and other parts of the coaches. Although to us the whole situation smacks of the comic, to these touchy gentlemen of the seventeenth century the matter was of great importance. In fact, Palma observes that if these gentlemen had been younger, blood probably would have been shed. Matters of less moment than this one often ended in violence.

Pasquines and Insulting Language

According to the honor code, the spoken or written insult was considered to be very serious. The *pasquín* is the Spanish equivalent of the American graffiti. In colonial times, criticisms of public officials and policies, and pointed accusations directed at influential people were commonplace. In a day when criticizing the authorities was prohibited, the *pasquines* were the delight of the community and it was not rare to find in them insults and reflections on honor. Trujillo, a city on the coast to the north of Lima, is the setting of a "tradición" entitled "Los pasquines del bachiller 'Pajalarga' " [The *Pasquines* of Longstraw the Bachelor], in which an author of insulting *pasquines* offended so many people and was so brazen about it that when the person thought to be guilty was apprehended, he was sentenced to die because he was considered the assassin of the honor of prominent people. His crime was so serious that his punishment was to serve as an example of how society obtained satisfaction for being insulted. He was to ride to the execution block on a donkey while someone accompanied him announcing the crime to the public. No heads were actually lost, however, because the accused was found innocent, and the guilty party escaped from Peru after being sentenced to die.

Violent indeed was the reaction of Don Diego to insulting verses in "El Nazareno." A certain versifier lampooned this gentleman, referring to him as continuously occupied in "desdoncellar doncellas" ("taking virginity from virgins"). Don Diego had two of his servants cudgel the poet severely and before the matter was concluded a lawsuit was brought against the touchy Don Diego. His complicity in the beating was not proved and therefore his accusers had to pay court costs and were ordered to satisfy Diego's wounded honor, for he had been insulted by the accusation. This satisfaction consisted of the accusers complying with Diego's request to meet him in a duel to the death. After Diego had killed three of his accusers, he allowed the rest of them to live after announcing that his reputation was free of taint.

Even viceroys became involved with *pasquines.* One of them, the Marquis of Cañete (1556–1561), replied in kind when a *pasquín* appeared on his palace wall stating that Cañete did not look like a viceroy, nor did he wear a viceroy's clothes, and that he should change his ways and observe the law. In the *pasquín* penned by the viceroy he acknowledged that it was possible that in appearance he did not seem to be a viceroy, but that he represented the king and enforced all laws. The ending of the poem made it clear that Cañete would not tolerate any more of these derogatory *pasquines* because in it he threatened to cut off some heads, presumably if more such verses were written. This *pasquín* was placed beneath the offending one and the warning was effective because no more *pasquines* directed against the marquis were seen ("Pasquín y contrapasquín").

Insulting spoken language is also a rich source of information about honor in Palma's narrations. Seven persons lost their lives in the "tradiciones" because of epithets and other insulting language. Some of the expressions which precipitated the violence include: "puerco"

("pig"), "pedazo de anticristo" ("you foul anti-Christ"), "tío Cal-
zones" (a beggar of the town), "miente usía" ("you lie"), and "puta"
("whore"). Several examples will be presented to demonstrate how
serious insulting language could be.

Francisco de Villacastín, one of the companions of Francisco
Pizarro, lost two of his front teeth when a monkey scored a direct hit
on his mouth with a coconut. Very sensitive about the incident and the
ensuing physical deformity, he allowed no one to jest about his teeth.
In this "tradición," "Don Alonso el Membrudo," we are told that
Don Alonso, a very strong man, said to him on one occasion, "My
dear sir, you only have the guts to have it out with a daring monkey
and come out of the fray snaggletoothed for the eternities." Villacastín's reply was to draw his sword and wound Don Alonso gravely in
the duel which followed.

Possibly one of the most bizarre cases deals with a young lady in
"Palabra suelta no tiene vuelta" [The Spoken Word Cannot be
Recalled] who married the governor of the city, a brigadier general
named Don Sebastián. Of course the fortunate suitor was careful to
watch his language among cultured people and especially when he was
in the presence of Manuelita, his aristocratic bride. Unfortunately, on
the night of his marriage his tongue was loosened by too much alcohol
and he said to his friends while he rested his hand on the neck of the
bride, "You rascals! I'm sure that my bride makes your mouths water
and that you really envy me for getting this precious thing! And you
should be envious because, *canario* [euphemism for an obscene word],
I'm carrying off with me the loveliest little whore in the city."
Manuelita gave him a scornful look and fled to her room, locking the
door behind her. Sebastián's head cleared immediately and he hurried
to her room to ask her forgiveness, but his bride turned a deaf ear to
his entreaties. After a year of separation she returned to her husband
on the condition that she be given satisfaction for the insult in a public
ball. The night of the function she dressed in her bride's gown and
joined the group when all the guests were present. When the time
came for her to take her husband's hand and walk to the center of the
room, she took him in her arms, whispering into his ear, "There are
offenses which call not for pardon, but for vengeance." With that she
drove a dagger into his heart and watched his lifeless body crumple to

the floor. Thus ends the piece; Palma refuses to tell us what happened to Manuelita. One point worthy of note in connection with this honor killing is that it took place in the nineteenth century, just eight years before independence. Even at that late date the subject of honor was a very touchy one and wounded honor could have tragic consequences.

The clergy could also strike back when they were dishonored, as we see in the "tradición" "Historia de una excomunión" [History of an Excommunication]. The dean of Cuzco had forbidden the wearing of trains to Mass and the archdean of that city became infuriated when a wealthy lady of the aristocracy went to Mass with her young daughter, who wore a dress with a yellow train. The lady defended herself, saying that she did not know the edict applied to girls as well as grown women. Undaunted, the archdean insisted that they be ejected from the cathedral. Thoroughly insulted, the lady started toward the door, muttering as she went, "Let's get out of here, daughter; it isn't right that we should continue to hear the insolent things this *zambo* [cross between Negro and Indian], donkey and dolt is saying." He then called her a pig because of the racial slur. Actually, says Palma, being called a donkey and a dolt was not serious. The next day the proud lady was excommunicated for insulting the archdean and interrupting Mass. She was not admitted back into the fold until she paid a fine of two hundred pesos and humbled herself sufficiently to ask his pardon.

In contrast to an extreme sensitivity about being insulted is the story about a contemporary of Palma in "Un Maquiavelo criollo" [A Creole Machiavelli], who subscribed to the philosophy that if he were insulted he would take no direct action against his offender, but rather permit him to continue on to the punishment he would one day receive. The protagonist, a doctor named Pajarito, was asked on one occasion to attend the sick son of the colonel of the battalion. He refused, knowing that his action would result in the loss of the promotion that he had earned. The colonel was the first to inform Pajarito of the loss of the promotion, claiming that he had told the president, "Pajarito doesn't know the first thing about being a physician." Pajarito's rejoinder left the colonel thunderstruck. "Thank you very much, colonel. I'm sure that what you said was right and proper. Patience." Pajarito's friends told him he had weak wine in his veins instead of blood but he merely told them he would be avenged some day. A few months later the colonel's body was seen hanging from a cathedral tower. He had been put to death because of traitorous activities and was proof to the physician that wounded honor is best satisfied by allowing human nature to take its course.

In conclusion, the following categories which involve insulting language are present in the "tradiciones": (1) sex (allusions to loose morals, impotence, or being cuckolded); (2) physical defects (allusions to being lame, blind, ugly, etc.); (3) race and religion (inferences that the individual concerned has Moorish or Jewish blood or that he has rejected the Catholic Church; (4) national pride (derogatory remarks about one's country or place of origin); (5) manly virtues (allusions to a lack of the qualities of forthright, virile manhood); (6) lack of respect for authority; and (7) other (all other language which denies an individual the respect he merits).

Honor and Slaps

The slap is perhaps the most insulting of all blows, for the attack is so personal, so degrading, and in many cases so shocking and humiliating that it must be avenged at all costs. In the "tradición" "Alonso de Toro" the protagonist was killed by his father-in-law because he had quarreled with his mother-in-law and had slapped her. The husband of the insulted woman ran the offender through without saying a word. Another piece in which a slap leads to dire consequences is "Los Incas ajedrecistas" [The Inca Chessplayers]. A chess match between Inca Manco, brother of the legitimate ruler, Huáscar, and Gómez Pérez, a conquistador, ended in death when the Inca claimed that a move made by the Spaniard was prohibited. Irate, Gómez Pérez called the Inca a pig and the Indian slapped him. Quickly the Spaniard drew his dagger and dispatched him with two blows. Very strange is the story of an aristocratic lady of Potosí in "Una vida por una honra" [Life for Honor]. She had been slapped during a dispute and she married a Biscayan under the condition that he would avenge the insult. When the husband continued to put off the day of retribution, his wife murdered him and tore out his heart. These three "tradiciones" demonstrate vividly how deeply sensibilities were injured when slaps were administered. In all three of them slaps were considered so insulting that either those who did the slapping were killed by the offended person or, as in the last piece, the wife killed her husband and tore out his heart when he failed to avenge a slap she had received.

Honor and Punishment Meted Out by the Authorities

To be imprisoned with commoners and to be whipped publicly were dishonorable for the man of honor. When nobles were required to go to prison they were incarcerated in a special jail or in a private home; thus, being shut up in a regular prison was a point of honor. In one narrative, "Capa colorada, caballo blanco y caja turún-tun-tun" [A Red Cape, a White Horse and a Rat-tat-tat Drum], Don Juan de Betanzos, doubly noble because his mother was an Inca princess and his father of noble lineage, was thrown into prison in Azángaro for defying the orders of the night patrol. The day after the arrest he was set free, but the damage had been done; he had been dishonored. He hid his shame in the mines of Arapa until he found a silver bull's head, which he sent to the king of Spain along with an account of the insult. The king accorded Betanzos certain privileges and named him a prince, whereupon he hastened to Azángaro to humble the alcalde who had incarcerated him. All of his plans for revenge came to naught because the alcalde, a Biscayan and thus noble by birth, resigned his post in order to avoid having to humble himself before Betanzos.

The outcome of the story above might have been grave if Betanzos had been able to confront the alcalde; in "Un asesinato justificado" [A Justified Killing] blood was shed over imprisonment. The principal character in this selection was not officially noble, but he must have considered himself to be because of the manner in which he avenged his lost honor. Tomás, a woodcutter, was sent to the penitentiary unjustly for a crime he did not commit and of which he was not accused. The alcalde had given a prisoner his liberty in return for the favors of his sister and had picked up the first poor devil he could find to take his place. Literally kidnapped and spirited away from Lima without being able to tell his wife and children of his fate, he spent eight years in prison savoring the revenge he would exact. Hurrying to Lima upon being released he waited for the alcalde at a bridge and knifed him to death. Then he performed an act reminiscent of Golden Age honor plays. He thrust his hands into the blood which gushed from the wound and bathed his head in it, exclaiming as he did so,"Now I have cleansed the white hair which grew while I was in prison at Chagres." The washing of hair appears to be the symbolic washing away of dishonor. Usually this purification was carried out by washing the place where the dishonor had been received; in this case the dishonor was conceived as being symbolized in the woodcutter's white hair, so it was his hair that was washed with blood. He was caught in the act and sentenced to the gallows; however, the viceroy sent the matter to the king, who decreed in 1769 that the killing of the alcalde had been justified and that the woodcutter was to be paid ten pesos a month for the injustice he had suffered. Why Tomás felt himself to be a man of honor is not certain, but one thing is clear, he definitely acted like one.

However, there is one "tradición," "¡A la cárcel todo Cristo!" [To Jail, Everyone!] which portrays the jailing of the viceroy himself. Don Ambrosio O'Higgins, viceroy of Peru during the end of the eighteenth century, became so concerned about disorders provoked by sons of some of the titled gentlemen of Lima that he gave orders that all troublemakers, regardless of nobility, be imprisoned. In spite of the instructions, his specially selected police captains continued to look the other way when sons of nobility were involved. Finally O'Higgins ordered that anyone on the streets after 10:00 P.M. be put into prison. One night the viceroy made an inspection tour to ascertain if his orders were being carried out. The first four of the five captains greeted him courteously; the fifth stopped him and, turning a deaf ear to his protestations, clapped him into jail as if he were an ordinary idler. The next day the four negligent captains lost their positions; their successors energetically carried out all their instructions.

Whippings figure in several "tradiciones." Two instances will be cited in which this cruel punishment caused dishonor. The first one is found in "Las orejas del alcalde" [The Mayor's Ears], one of Palma's most popular pieces. A soldier, Don Cristóbal de Agüero, the son of an alderman in Seville, was a poor *hidalgo*. He and the alcalde both courted the same young woman and it was the soldier who won her heart. How delighted the alcalde was when one night he found the soldier had been arrested for gambling and was to be whipped with twelve lashes for gambling for he was too poor to pay the fine!

According to law the guilty party was to be whipped with twelve lashes if he could not pay the one hundred *duros* fine. Don Cristóbal protested that he was an *hidalgo* and could not be whipped, but the alcalde merely mocked him and said, "¡Hidalgo, hidalgo! Cuéntamelo por la otra oreja" (*Hidalgo! Hidalgo!* Tell me again, in the other ear). Angrily the soldier swore that if the whipping was carried out he would avenge himself on the ears of the alcalde. The whipping was then carried out in the presence of the alcalde and four of his men. After being whipped the hidalgo was released from prison, but before leaving he told the jailer to warn the alcalde that his ears actually belonged to Cristóbal, who was loaning them to his persecutor for one year. The next day Don Cristóbal presented himself to his captain and asked for a leave of absence because he had lost his honor. The captain acceded to the soldier's request.

Three months later Cristóbal began to wage psychological warfare against the alcalde by accosting him unexpectedly day and night and making remarks about "his" ears. The war of nerves had the desired effect on the alcalde, who trembled at the slightest sound and saw the image of the soldier wherever he went. Even when the alcalde went to Lima on business the soldier confronted him at every stop along the way to make sure that the ears were in their proper place. Finally, exactly one year after the whipping, Cristóbal slipped into the alcalde's room, tied him to a chair, and after telling him that he had come to avenge his honor, sliced off his ears. Cristóbal then fled to Spain, where Charles the Fifth granted him an audience, pardoned him, and named him captain of a regiment being formed in Mexico. The alcalde died a month after the attack, more from the fear of being called "The Earless One" than as a result of the wounds he had sustained.

An interesting sidelight related to the gravity of whippings is the fact that certain schools in Lima provided that "condesitos" and "marquesitos" were not to be whipped for not knowing their lessons or for committing infractions of the teachers' rules. These privileged lads were to be accompanied by Negro boys from their own households who suffered the whipping merited by their masters ("La endemoniada") [The Possessed]. These "tradiciones" make it apparent that when a nobleman was placed in a public prison or whipped he felt that he had lost his honor. The case of Viceroy O'Higgins presents, however, an interesting contrast. His incarceration took place toward the end of the eighteenth century, when attitudes were becoming more liberal. In order to restore order to Lima he ordered young nobles to be imprisoned and to make his point more forcefully allowed himself, the viceroy of Peru, to be placed in public prison. Also, it appears that even commoners felt that their honor had been stained when they were sentenced to prison for crimes they did not commit. At least this was so in the case of the woodcutter in "Un asesinato justificado" [A Justified Killing], who not only killed the alcalde who sent him to prison but washed his hair in the official's blood to wash away the shame and dishonor of the eight years of unjustified incarceration.

The Word of Honor

The importance of keeping one's word of honor can hardly be overemphasized. In theory a promise was sacred and had to be kept in spite of possible harm to the one who made it or to his loved ones. A man of honor who failed to keep his word lost his honor, regardless of the circumstances.

A famous pirate, Richard Hawkins, owed his life to a promise made by the man who took him prisoner. "Las querellas de San Toribio" [Saint Toribio's Disputes] narrates what happened after Hawkins was captured by Don Beltrán de Castro after a running battle of several days and was promised by him that he would not be put to death. The *audiencia* ignored the promise by Beltrán de Castro and sentenced Hawkins to the gallows. But the Spanish commander, feeling that his honor was at stake, appealed to the king, who ruled in favor of leniency.

Another revealing example of the keeping of one's word of honor is narrated in "La bofetada póstuma" [The Posthumous Slap]. Captain Luis Perdomo, a loyal follower of Viceroy Núñez de Vela, sought to borrow money from a merchant without any security except his word in order to equip a company for battle. When the merchant refused the loan of 1,000 ducats, Perdomo plucked some whiskers from his beard and said, "How would it be if I made a pledge of these honorable whiskers for eight days?" After this the merchant lent him the money because he had faith in an honorable man's resolve to keep his word.

A more dramatic incident, which involves a priest's determination to honor his vows to keep the secrets of the confessional, is found in "El secreto de confesión." The two principal characters in the piece are Father Marieluz, a loyal supporter of the king, and Don Ramón Rodil, commander of the Spanish forces shortly before the battle of Ayacucho. Rodil learned that some of his soldiers were planning to revolt against him and had them shot. Not convinced that he had taken care of all the conspirators, he demanded that Marieluz reveal what had been told him in the confessional concerning the revolt. The priest's reply was, "My general, you are asking the impossible of me, for I would not sacrifice the salvation of my soul by revealing the secret of a penitent person. I would not do it even though the king himself, may the good Lord preserve him, gave the order." Rodil, angry at the firm resolve of the priest, ordered that he divulge the secrets or prepare to be shot as a traitor. Marieluz defended his decision, remarking that he would prefer to be a traitor to his king than to his God. Exasperated, Rodil brought four soldiers into the room and gave the order that sent four bullets ripping into the kneeling Father Pedro Marieluz.

One "tradición" narrates a story in which a man is killed because he failed to do some work on time. In "Un general de antaño" [A General of Olden Times] a captain of the royal army ordered a new uniform from a tailor, who promised it would be ready within eight days. The captain wanted it for a gala ball and was especially anxious to make a good impression. As the days went by and the uniform was not delivered the captain grew uneasy. On the eighth day, with the ball two days away, the tailor promised again that the uniform would be ready. At eight o'clock the night of the dance, the captain, still without his new uniform, met the tailor in the company of a girl of the streets. When the captain reproached him, the tailor merely said that everyone knew that promises made by tailors were not always kept because sometimes it was impossible to fulfill them. Even though it was just a tailor's promise that had been broken, the captain marched him to a nearby square and shot him at point-blank range. As far as this son of aristocratic parents was concerned, all promises were to be kept.

Spanish honor required that promises be kept, even though, as in the case of Richard Hawkins, a military commander had given his word to a pirate. When the *audiencia* sentenced Hawkins to the gallows in spite of Beltrán de Castro's promise, the sentence was appealed by the latter to the king, whose decision upheld the promise made to a buccaneer. A priest is executed when he refuses to tell secrets of the confessional he had promised not to reveal; a tailor is shot because he makes promises he makes little effort to keep; and a captain obtains a loan from a merchant when he pledges, along with his word, some whiskers from his beard. Such "tradiciones" give us some insight into the importance placed on keeping one's word.

Honor and Women

In the Hispanic tradition the reputation of women was to be preserved unsullied at all costs. Immoral conduct or even the suspicion of it could lead to harsh punishment. Thus, a man of honor was obligated to guard the reputation of a sweetheart, wife, daughter, female relative, or even a female ward. According to the theoretical code of honor a man had the right to kill the offending female and the man with whom she was involved. Honor plays such as Calderón de la Barca's *El médico de su honra* [The Physician of His Honor] and *A secreto agravio, secreta venganza* [For a Secret Offense, Secret Vengeance] are good examples of the severity with which indiscretions were punished in Spain. Palma's "tradiciones" run the gamut from honor killings in the strict tradition to the ignoring of the punishment of the guilty parties. In this discussion these cases of honor will be divided into two categories: (1) honor and married women; and (2) honor and unmarried women.

In four "tradiciones" husbands resort to violent action. "El encapuchado" [The Hooded Man] is the bizarre tale of a husband who charged his brother with guarding his honor while he made a business trip to Spain. Unfortunately, while he was away his brother began to make love to the businessman's wife; when the latter was informed of his dishonor by letter he returned home immediately. But instead of taking action quickly he roamed the streets of Lima after curfew for seven years dressed as a priest, terrorizing the residents of his neighborhood. His wife and brother were unaware of his return to Lima until the cuckold burst into the room where they were holding a birthday party for her, and slew his wife and brother on the spot. He then told the whole story to the authorities, who fined him because he had worn the sacred robes of a priest. Since the honor killing was justified, he was exonerated and allowed to leave for Spain. The husband's honor had been lost when he became a cuckold; therefore violent means of regaining his honor were justified. The tribunals of the period were fully aware of the importance of honor and refused to punish the husband who had killed in order to regain his place in a society which placed profound importance on honor. It should be noted, however, that if the guilty parties were of high rank, i.e., the upper nobility or royalty, severe punishment of the person who committed the honor murder or murders could take place. Indeed, circumstances altered cases.

"Cortar por lo sano" [Take Resolute Action] ends in the death of a wife and her suspected lover, in this case a priest. Corvalán, a resident of Ica, feared for his honor because his wife was confessing too much to a certain priest, so he went to the *corregidor* for advice. He was told to take resolute action, which puzzled Corvalán. Upon returning home he saw the priest leaving his home and immediately stabbed him to death. He was imprisoned and hanged in spite of his claim that he was merely following the advice of the *corregidor*. The protagonist in a short portion of "Muerta en vida" [Dead While Alive] made a pact with the Devil that the latter would have his soul if he could kill his wife and the priest with whom she was committing adultery. After he had killed the two adulterers, he hanged himself. This complete account appears in one short paragraph in the "tradición." We know nothing about the protagonist except that he was a Chilean and performed the deeds noted. We do not even know if he was a nobleman. It appears that his principal concern was to gain revenge and he was willing to sell his soul in order to realize his goal. No thought of regaining his place in society is found here, possibly because he would have to take the life of a priest. Men of the cloth were ordinarily considered incapable of wounding another person's honor, thus the chance would be remote that the husband could be exonerated for the killing of the priest because it was not an honor killing in the strict sense of the word.

A very strange type of honor revenge is portrayed in "El niño llorón" [The Crying Child]. Urbistondo, a shoemaker, had to make trips to nearby villages and while he was absent his wife would make love to someone. One day when he was preparing to take a trip he charged a figurine of the Child Jesus with preserving his honor, promising to break its leg if it failed. Upon returning home he learned that his wife had fled with her lover, whereupon the shoemaker picked up an awl and drove it into the figurine's leg. The Child Jesus began to cry out in pain and blood oozed from the leg of the figurine. Urbistondo, shaken by the experience, did not seek further honor revenge but spent his remaining days in a monastery.

In the "tradiciones" some husbands react much more calmly when they find out they are being cuckolded. In "¿Quién toca el arpa?" [Who Is Playing the Harp?] the husband does nothing at all in spite of the fact that night after night his wife entertains various lovers while he plays his harp and drinks his liquor. Whether he knew what his wife was doing is not clear, but her suspicious conduct did not seem to bother him in the least. It is apparent that this husband held very liberal views with respect to honor. According to the code he was obligated to know of his wife's whereabouts at all times in order to make it very unlikely she might be alone with a man in a compromising situation. And even though nothing improper might occur, there is always the question of the "qué dirán" or what people might say. If people said that an individual had lost his honor, in effect he did lose his honor. None of these considerations seems to have been of any importance to the husband in this "tradición." Another "tradición," entitled "La carta de 'La Libertadora' " [The Letter of "La Libertadora"], tells of a shopkeeper who grew tired of his wife's amorous adventures and upbraided her severely, threatening to take violent action if she did not mend her ways. Her behavior did not change so he took the case to court, something which was highly unusual in matters of honor, and asked for a divorce. The divorce was not granted, whereupon he solved the matter by leaving town. Obviously honor was not very important to this man. He publicized the infidelity of his wife when he took the case to court instead of shedding her blood, which another cuckolded husband might have done. He left his wife when the divorce was not granted because he could no longer live with a woman who had wronged him in the past and would probably continue to cuckold him.

The final case in this section deals with Manuela Sáenz, "La Libertadora," who appears in the "tradición" mentioned above. Manuela left her husband to become the lover of Simón Bolívar and was quite irritated when he continued to try to persuade her to return to him. Finally, she wrote to him, telling him she was content to live with Bolívar as his mistress even though society would condemn her for it. She felt that she was just as honorable living with Bolívar without benefit of marriage as she would have been living with her husband. Instead of seeking revenge for his lost honor, the husband didn't do anything. This "tradicíon" is proof that not all husbands whose wives were unfaithful exacted bloody vengeance. For some, stained honor, or perhaps more accurately, what might have been considered stained honor by some people, did not require bloody action.

Palma portrays fathers and brothers as deeply concerned with the reputation of daughters or sisters, but in not one instance does a girl suffer death when her father or brother discovers that her actions have dishonored the family name. In two "tradiciones," however, we see what fathers do when the reputation of their daughters is besmirched. In one of the episodes already related in "El Nazareno" a young girl was seduced by a libertine and then abandoned. The public dishonor weighed so heavily on the parents that when the seducer left town, thus making marriage impossible, they lost their minds.

"Un drama íntimo" [An Intimate Drama] could almost have been penned by Cervantes because it is so tenderly written and is so full of a humanistic approach to life. Laurentina, the young daughter of a marquis, preferred marriage to life in a convent, so arrangements were made for her to marry the son of a count who was a friend of his. This pleased both Baldomero, the son, and Laurentina, but the young scoundrel took advantage of the lack of experience of the marquis's daughter, seduced her, and then left her for another. Feeling herself debased, Laurentina threw herself into the arms of her father and wept. The marquis wrote to Baldomero demanding an explanation. The cynical reply read as folllows, "A daughter of such loose morals would become an adulterous wife." Certain that the young man was lying he showed the letter to Laurentina, who freely admitted her guilt and asked her father to forgive her. The marquis, instead of vilifying her and killing her, held her in his arms and whispered, "My poor angel" as he wiped a tear away. Sometime later the marquis challenged Baldomero to a duel; when the haughty young man refused satisfaction, the marquis plunged a dagger into Baldomero's chest. He then went directly to the alcalde, to whom he admitted the murder. Tried and about to be sentenced to death, the marquis would reveal nothing about the motive for his crime. To save her father, Laurentina sent Baldomero's insulting letter to the viceroy, who had the count read it. The latter, upon recognizing the handwriting, fell into a chair with his hands covering his face and said, "The marquis acted within his rights. [My son] deserved to die." The marquis was absolved of the crime and none of the details of the case was ever given to the public.

We do find cases in which the brother of a wronged woman kills the seducer and some cases in which the women kill the men who have abandoned them. The former type is represented by "El verdugo real de Cuzco" [The Royal Executioner of Cuzco] and "Justos y pecadores" [The Righteous and the Sinners]. In both of them the girl took the veil and the brother put the seducer to death. The type in which the women kill their faithless lovers is seen in "Una vida por una honra" [A Life in Exchange for Honor]. The principal story of this piece tells of a young lady who became the victim of a young swain when he promised to marry her. Tiring of the affair, her lover fled to Potosí, where he thought he would be free of her. Not the type to live with her dishonor, Claudia followed him to the mining city dressed as a man. After gambling with him and even lending him money she told him to meet her in Regocijo Square to return the money. When she met him, she threw his faithlessness in his teeth, challenged him to a duel, and killed him on the spot. The same "tradición" tells of two sisters who killed two brothers in Potosí, presumably for the same reason. The battle was fought with lances and on horseback, and after the dust of the conflict had settled, the brothers were dead. Palma makes a wry comment on the sensitivity of the women of Potosí with respect to honor. First, he says: "Zambomba

con las mujercitas de Potosí," which can be roughly translated as "To
Hell with the young women of Potosí." Then he says: "Fortunately
her [Claudia's] example and that of the two vengeful sisters were not
contagious, for if Eve's daughters had taken it into their minds to
challenge all the men who had seduced them and then abandoned
them, surely this world would find out that all the men had
disappeared."

In Palma's treatment of honor in which women are involved we see
that the punishment required by the honor code was not always meted
out. The "tradiciones" are not Golden Age plays but rather a
reflection of every-day life in Peru and thus, though there were
occasions when honor was cleansed by the shedding of blood, there
were others in which women whose actions clouded their husbands'
honor were not punished in any way. In many cases Palma gives us
scant information about the characters involved in his "tradiciones"
dealing with the honor of women, but in my research I have discovered
that most of the examples of severe punishment are found in
"tradiciones" set in the sixteenth and seventeenth centuries and that
the dishonored man was of the nobility. Social station and the period
in which the events took place were important in how the provisions of
the code of honor were applied.

The Catholic Church

Undoubtedly there was no institution more powerful and omnipresent in the Peru of the colonial period than the Catholic Church, and
there are more "tradiciones" in which ecclesiastical matters constitute
the theme than there are of any other topic. It should be remembered
that Palma's first significant published work was *Los anales de la
Inquisición de Lima* [Annals of the Inquisition of Lima], a piece of
research which for many years was considered to be the only historical
treatise dealing with that infamous tribunal. From that investigation
Palma extracted much information that later became the starting point
for his "tradiciones." The treatment provided portrays the Church as
Palma saw it, with emphasis on some of the more striking aspects of
the role the Church and the clergy played in old Peru.

Palma did not come out in open opposition to the Church, but his
critical attitude toward the institution is apparent. Well known is his

hostility toward the Jesuits, exemplified by the following from "Entre jesuitas, agustinianos y dominicos" [Among Jesuits, Augustinians and Dominicans]: "The incontrovertible fact is that in Peru the Jesuits have always been battlers and rioters, insolent toward authority and sowers of discord." He referred to them as "the feared disciples of Loyola" and said of them: "Un jesuita y una suegra saben más que una culebra" ("A Jesuit and a mother-in-law know more than a serpent"). He does not seem to display this attitude toward any other religious order.

One of the strongest comments concerning the Church appears in "Supersticiones de los peruanos" [Superstitions of the Peruvian People, (1891)]: "Only by civilizing people and causing reason to overcome faith can superstition be killed. When superstition disappears, then will the prestige of Papal Rome also disappear. Its omnipotence is founded on an ignorance which enslaves the great majority of society." In the same piece we also find the following:

[Indians] do not distinguish between God and the priest, who exploits them as he wishes. It can be said that they work only for him and everything they earn ends up in the simoniac pocket of the Catholic priest. And we omit the abuses of the confessional, which if infinite in civilized places, among these semibarbarians are worse than the imagination can conceive.

There are villages where brides are deposited in the home of the priest eight days before the marriage and it shocks no one that he exercises his right of *pernada* [the right to initiate the bride in her sexual duties] just like the feudal lords of long ago. (Aguilar, p. 1434)

Palma derives great satisfaction from writing about miracles and the appearance of demons and gently smiles at the naiveté of people who believed in such things. With respect to miracles he says for example: "The Franciscan chronicle relates this [event] differently. It says that Friar Gómez, in order to escape from his admirers, rose up in the air and flew from the bridge to the tower of his *convent*. I do not deny it and I do not affirm it. Perhaps it happened and perhaps it didn't. With respect to miracles I must say that I don't waste ink defending or refuting them." ("El alacrán de fray Gómez" [Friar Gómez's Scorpion]).[3] One other remark which reveals his irreverent attitude toward the Church is this: "We know of only one mine that has produced more silver than the mines of Potosí. That mine is called Purgatory. Since the Church invented or discovered Purgatory, it has fashioned a large chest without a bottom which will never be filled. In it are thrown alms offered by the faithful in Masses, indulgences, [money for] prayers for the dead and other goodies which departed souls are so fond of" ("Una vida por una honra" [A Life in Exchange for Honor]) (Aguilar, p. 371).

For Palma, in 1571 Spain was one great convent and the same could be said of the Americas. Rich families spent great sums of money on monastic foundations and every family felt that to have many friars and many nuns was to have a special little place reserved for them in Heaven. In 1768 he notes that in Lima alone there were 1,300 friars and 700 nuns.

Miracles

One of the most fascinating of the miracle makers we meet in the pages of the "tradiciones" is Friar Gómez, who lived in Lima from 1587 to 1631. He was a refectionary in the hospital of the Franciscans, a lay member whose life of devotion caused papers to be sent to Rome requesting he be canonized, a request which was not granted. Of Friar Gómez Palma wrote: "In my land Friar Gómez performed miracles in wholesale lots, without being aware of them, and without really caring about them. He was just a miracle monger, like the fellow who spoke in prose without realizing it."

The first two of the three miracles Palma reports are digressions in the piece entitled "Friar Gómez's Scorpion," one of Palma's most beloved "tradiciones." It seems that one day Gómez was crossing a bridge when a horse threw its rider; as a result the man lay bleeding with his skull fractured. The cry went up to find someone who could administer the last rites, but Gómez leaned over the stricken man, put the cord of his habit on his mouth, pronounced three blessings and then, with no help from doctors or medicine, the wounded fellow got up and acted as if nothing had happened to him. The crowd which had congregated tried to carry the Friar off in triumph, but Gómez ran away from them and shut himself up in his cell. The chronicle of the Franciscans is not quite in agreement with the latter part of the account, for it states that Gómez flew to his *convent*.[4] The second of these miracles took place when on that same day Gómez went to the hospital and there found Saint Francisco Solano suffering from a severe migraine headache. Gómez took his pulse and told him he must eat something because he was very weak. The Saint replied that he had no appetite, but Gómez stubbornly insisted that he would have to have something to eat. Finally, in order to quiet the Friar, Solano said he would eat some *pejerreyes* (a species of mackerel). Of course he was attempting to be facetious because these fish were out of season. Nothing daunted, Gómez reached into the left sleeve of his habit and pulled out two *pejerreyes* which were as fresh as if they had just been taken from the ocean. Gómez fried them, Saint Francisco Solano ate them and was cured on the spot.

The principal miracle in this piece is about an honorable peddler who one day requested that Gómez lend him 500 *duros* because everyone else had turned a deaf ear to his petition. Gómez was amazed at the entreaty because he was as poor as the proverbial church mouse, but the peddler insisted that the good Friar could help him because he had faith that he would not leave him disconsolate. Said Gómez, "Your faith will save you. Wait a moment." Noticing a scorpion on the wall he captured it in a piece of paper and handed it to the peddler, reminding him that it must be returned within six months, the period of the loan. Hurrying to a money lender, the peddler opened up the paper and the scorpion had been transformed into a splendid work of art, a scorpion whose body was a huge emerald mounted on gold and whose head was a magnificent diamond with two rubies for eyes. The money lender coveted the precious jeweled pin and offered to lend the peddler 2,000 *duros,* but the latter was content to borrow the 500 *duros.* After six months the money was paid back and the pin redeemed. The peddler returned it to Gómez, who placed it on the splay of the window and then told the scorpion to continue on its way, whereupon the pin became a scorpion and walked away. In such a fashion Palma portrays a Peruvian friar who performed miracles by the score according to monastery records studied by the traditionist. Here we see the complete faith a merchant had in Gómez's ability to help him, the miraculous powers Gómez possessed, and the determination of the merchant to use the splendid jewel exclusively for the purpose for which he had asked Friar Gómez's help. All of this is enhanced by a slightly irreverent style which makes this "tradición" one of Palma's most beautiful.

The tenth viceroy of Peru, the Count of Monterrey, reigned from 1604 to 1606, a period during which so many miracles were allegedly performed that the count was called the "Viceroy of the Miracles," none of which he himself accomplished. One striking miracle deals with a woman who needed money in order to marry her two daughters properly. At wits end she decided to appeal to a wealthy merchant for help. She wrote a letter to him in which she asked that he send her in gold what the letter itself weighed. Amused, the merchant placed the letter on one pan of a scale and began to place gold on the other. One ounce and the letter was heavier, then more and more ounces and the letter refused to rise even a minute amount. Finally, when the sum reached 1,000 pesos the pan on which the letter was resting rose. The merchant, convinced that Heaven was on the side of the lady, gave her the money and the proud mother presented her daughters with a substantial dowry.

The other outstanding miracle helped an errant wife escape her husband's wrath. The episode took place in Potosí and it occurred when the wife found herself in sore straits because her husband, having been given advance information about his spouse's tryst, returned home when her lover was present. The latter hid under some furniture in the bedroom and the wife entreated the blessed souls of Purgatory to aid her. When the husband, dagger in hand, burst into the room he saw only some ladies visiting with his wife. Certain that she owed her life to souls from the other world, she mended her ways and paid for Masses and suffrages for souls in Purgatory ("El Virrey de los Milagros" [The Viceroy of the Miracles]).

The greatest of all the miracle workers in Peru was, it was said, Fray Martín de Porres, whom Palma said he would compare with any European saint. The lay brother performed so many miracles that the Prior of the Dominicans had to forbid him to continue *milagreando* (Palma's word, which means to perform miracles). One day Porres was walking by a scaffold when a workman fell from it. The worker had fallen twelve of the twenty-four feet to the ground when Porres stopped him in mid-air. Not wishing to disobey the prior, Martín ran to find him in order to ask permission to complete the miracle. The prior was somewhat irritated because a miracle had already been performed, so he told Porres to finish up his miracle, but to be careful that he indulge in no more of them. This incident is noteworthy for several reasons. The miracle of saving a human being from death or at least serious injury is caricatured by having Friar Martín stop the falling worker in mid-air and then leaving him suspended while he asks permission to save his life. The Catholic Church is thus depicted as an institution which could restrict miracles, regardless of the good they might accomplish, and which could make the weighty decision concerning whether a person involved in an accident should fall or be saved. And what if the prior had not given permission for the completion of the miracle? We are left to speculate on that point without any help from Palma.

The following miracles further attest to the great powers of Friar Martín. According to a panegyric printed in 1863, Porres was in the Molucca Islands, China and Japan without leaving Lima because God granted him the privilege of bilocation. On another occasion the lay brother was sent to obtain a sugar loaf for the infirmary. Perhaps he had insufficient money to buy refined sugar. Whatever the case, the prior reproved him for bringing unrefined sugar. Porres told him not to get upset, for he would wash it. No sooner said than done, he submerged the loaf in the water in the baptismal font and when he took it out it was white and dry. Finally, Palma tells of the miracle of the mice, animals which were unknown in Peru until the Spaniards unwittingly carried some of them to the land of the Incas in 1552 in a cargo of codfish. The Indians called them *hucuchas,* which means animals that come from the sea. When Friar Martín was a youth there were still relatively few of the rodents in Peru, but by the time he was a lay member they were overrunning the monastery. Traps failed to get rid of them so Porres caught one and promised it that if the mice would leave the monastery and live in the orchard he would feed all of them every day. The arrangement was satisfactory for the mice and Porres carried out his word. But one mouse must have forgotten the pact because one day he decided that the odor coming from the food prepared for the dog and cat was too tantalizing. Porres had succeeded in having the natural enemies, the cat and dog, eat together in harmony but now the uninvited guest was threatening to destroy that peaceful order. Porres reproved them and invited the mouse to eat with the other animals. From that day on the dog, the cat, and the mouse ate together in love and friendship. Palma took great delight in writing about miracles. They were an integral part of Peru's past and provided a flavor which helped the traditionist bring life and vigor to times of yore. He prefers not to take a position concerning their veracity; rather, he presents tales about miracles in a tongue-in-cheek fashion, permitting the reader to draw his own conclusions ("El porqué fray Martín de Porres, santo limeño, no hace ya milagros" [Why the Lima Saint Friar Martín de Porres Doesn't Perform Miracles Any More]).

Excommunications

That many excommunications were pronounced in Peru is clear from the "tradiciones," but to what extent they were feared is not; in fact, Palma is ambivalent, saying in one piece that they were completely harmless and in another that a person threatened with excommunication trembled in his shoes. In "Entre jesuitas, agustinianos y dominicos" [Among Jesuits, Augustinians and Dominicans, (1886)] we read the following:

> In those days excommunications ran rampant and produced less effect than the powders of Jalapa, a laxative then in use. The Inquisition excommunicated, bishops and cathedral chapters excommunicated, priests excommunicated, superiors of monastic orders excommunicated; in short every cleric who wore a habit had the right to declare his neighbor outside of the communion of the Apostolic Church of Rome, condemning him to the eternal fires of Hell. For the most insignificant things, for a doubt of conscience, for having a mistress, for reading a prohibited book, for not fasting during Lent, there fell upon an individual an excommunication which cut him off at the hypotenuse [in other words, he was completely cut off from the Church]. It can be stated without exaggeration that two-thirds of the Peruvians lived in excommunication. It appears that excommunications caused them to have good health; they didn't take away sleep or appetite. Even viceroys were excommunicated and they kept on governing as if nothing had happened. (Aguilar, p. 215)

However, "Dos excomuniones" [Two Excommunications], published in 1891, reveals a completely different attitude. Palma states:

"In those days an excommunication did not weigh *adarmes* [one-sixth of an ounce] like the ones of our day and age, but tons. Today excommunications resemble zarzuelas in that they give rise to noisy street fun and bring profitable popularity for the excommunicated. They do not take away sleep or appetite. I know people who are dying to have the sentence of excommunication fall upon them." In the latter "tradición" two cases are related in which excommunications were certainly feared. In one story a gentleman by the name of Don Juan de Aliaga y Sotomayor, grandson of the conquistador Jerónimo de Aliaga, married an aristocratic lady who brought a dowry of 50,000 *duros* to her wedding. After twelve years of marriage, the lady died, bequeathing all her money and property to Don Juan under the stipulation that he establish a fund for the benefit of the choir in the metropolitan. The years went by and Don Juan showed not the slightest interest in setting up the fund, a sin of omission which was very displeasing to certain persons who would benefit from the money provided. Finally they took the case to court, but Don Juan's lawyer was so skillful that the case dragged on interminably. His patience at an end, the archbishop ordered that the widower be excommunicated. When this happened Don Juan was in the process of marrying again, but when his intended learned of the penalty inflicted she refused to see him or write to him. Don Juan cared not a whit about being excommunicated, but the attitude of his future wife forced him to change his mind. Defeated, he set up the fund and was then married shortly thereafter.

The protagonists of the other story, in which excommunication is merely threatened, are the bishop and the alcalde of Huamanga. A conflict arose between them when the alcalde arrested the owner of a store where liquor and other merchandise were sold because the owner refused to observe the curfew. The bishop was upset because the owner of the store was his neighbor and one of the doors of his residence led to the store; therefore he felt that the storekeeper should have immunity from the law. The alcalde sent a letter to the bishop to explain matters but López Roldán, the ecclesiastic, called the alcalde names and threatened to excommunicate him if the owner of the store was not released. And in the process the angry López Roldán had called the scribe who brought the letter some choice names. His pride wounded, the scribe protested that he was not involved in the matter and did not deserve such treatment. Even more enraged, the bishop called him a heretic and ordered him to leave, promising to excommunicate him also if he should utter a word. At that the scribe beat a hasty retreat. Palma then writes the following: "Would you believe that the alcalde of Huamanga, Don Nicolás de Boza y Solís, trembled like a rat and set the prisoner at liberty? Well, that is exactly what happened." It is obvious that the threat of excommunication was frightening to some, even causing a mayor to release a wrong-doer rather than suffer such heavy punishment.

Strange indeed were the circumstances which could lead to an excommunication. "Una excomunión famosa" [A Famous Excommunication] narrates what happened when a thief stole from Don Antonio de Ribera one of the first three starts of grape vines to be planted in Peru. This happened in the year 1561. Apprised of the theft Ribera spared no effort attempting to find out who the thief was, but in vain. He then appealed to the archbishop, who went through all the necessary rites and then pronounced the penalty of *excomunión mayor* on the thief. Three years later a gentleman from Valparaíso asked to confess to the archbishop, who was surprised to learn that on the other side of the confessional grille was the thief of the grapevine. During these three years his excommunication had worried him and now he had returned to Lima to make restitution. The archbishop agreed to lift the sentence if he replaced the start with the same mystery with which he had stolen the original one several years ago. The thief complied with the conditions, placing a pouch of 1,000 *duros* at the foot of the start. Not content with the gesture, he left a letter in which he asked Ribera to forgive him and made a contribution of 2,000 *duros* to the Hospital of Santa Ana, which the archbishop was having constructed. As a footnote, Palma points out that the original start had cost half a *peseta* in Seville. To be excommunicated was of such a serious nature that, according to the events portrayed in this piece, the thief, who in all probability would never have been found out, gave 3,000 *duros* in order to persuade the archbishop to lift the sentence. Even though three years had passed, it is evident that the weight of the excommunication bore down heavily upon him.

Some of the most interesting examples of the imposing of this sanction portray the excommunication of ecclesiastics, and in a "tradición" previously cited, "Among Jesuits, Augustinians and Dominicans," we see clergymen excommunicating each other. A serious conflict arose in Cuzco in 1589 when some doggerel critical of a Jesuit, Father Lucio Garcete, was being circulated by the Augustinians and Dominicans. The Jesuits presented the case to Don Luis de Olivera, an ecclesiastical judge, who tried to find out who the author of the verses was. In addition he threatened with excommunication those who had read the scandalous material. Many who were fearful of the dread punishment came forward to confess their sin; the number included seven clerics, twenty-seven friars, and one nun. Intense questioning drew out the fact that the author of the doggerel was Friar Juan Gutiérrez of the Augustinian Order. Gutiérrez was ordered imprisoned in his monastery but the prior of the Augustinians did everything he could to prevent the order from being carried out. Certain that he had committed no wrong against the Church Gutiérrez appealed his case to the cathedral chapter. Olivera ruled in favor of the Jesuits, but the chapter refused to proclaim the decision. Then Olivera threatened to excommunicate the chapter and its leaders threatened to do the same to Olivera. Supporters of Gutiérrez went to Olivera's home to place him under some kind of arrest, but the latter had fled, leaving posted on the wall the announcement of the excommunication of Friar Juan Gutiérrez. The friar's supporters took down those announcements and posted in their place announcements of the excommunication of Don Luis de Olivera. Faced with a situation which could erupt into a minor civil war because feelings on both sides were running high, the civil authorities brought the two sides together and the case was sent to Lima, where the Audiencia ruled in favor of the Jesuits. The final disposition of the excommunications which had been declared will have to remain in limbo because Palma states that at this point the document he was studying came to an end. The grotesqueness of this episode is enhanced by the fact that people could be excommunicated, or in other ways cut off from the Church and sentenced to eternal damnation for such trivial matters. In addition Palma seems to delight in portraying ecclesiastics as if they were petulant children. The climax in this comic operetta is reached when the Audiencia has to decide the matter or face the possibility of the eruption of a civil war. Palma seems to be chuckling at man's frailties, especially those of men whose spiritual vocation should place them above such trifling matters.

Ecclesiastical Elections

Elections of ecclesiastical officers and even of patron saints very often led to confrontations which kept cities in a state of commotion for days. One of the chief rivalries which caused hostilities was the competition between *peninsulares* (those fortunate enough to be born in Spain), who always wanted one of their number to be elected, and *criollos* (born of Spanish parents, but in the New World), who wanted one of their number to receive that honor. "Un virrey capitulero" [A Capitular Viceroy] tells the history of this type of rivalry in the seventeenth century. The bitterly fought election of the provincial of the Augustinians in 1669 had its origins in the previous election in which a *criollo,* a wealthy Peruvian named Diego de Urrutia, had won the election by one vote. Since the *peninsulares* and the *criollos* saw in such elections a question of national honor, the vigor with which the campaigns were carried out can be understood. The *criollos* celebrated this victory with great holidays and celebrations because for the first time the Spaniards had not prevailed. While Urrutia was still provincial, a new viceroy arrived who took a dislike to Urrutia because of the latter's brother, Jerónimo, who had aided the governor of Panama after the viceroy had imprisoned him. Determined that the Spaniards would again possess the highest authority in the *convent,* the viceroy, Don Pedro de Castro y Andrade, Count of Lemos, began to meddle in the election process. He completely controlled the situation by doing several things. First, he persuaded the Spaniards to unite behind Father Lagunilla, one of his friends, and then he had the provincial, Diego de Urrutia, and four of the latter's most devoted supporters sent to Callao under armed guard. The viceroy then entered the capitular chambers and instructed the members of the order to vote. Two more *criollos* were removed when they tried to obstruct the election, and then the election began. In order to guarantee that there would be no further disturbances, the viceroy and the Audiencia stayed in the convent from 4:00 P.M. to 5:00 A.M., when the announcement was made that Lagunilla had triumphed. Here we see the importance of national honor and personal prejudices in ecclesiastical elections. We also see that the viceroy did not hesitate to perform illegal acts and to take upon himself ecclesiastical authority in order to gain his ends.

Elections for nuns also led to strife on some occasions. In fact, Palma tells us that in 1634 Ana María de Frías stabbed another nun to death over the question of an election ("Vítores" [Bravos]). The longest narrative portraying the election of a mother superior is "Las clarisas de Trujillo" [The Clares of Trujillo]. ("Clares" refers to nuns of a particular order, the Poor Clares). In an election held in 1786 the provincial used all of his influence to have Mother Casanova elected. However, she was only thirty-three years old and the other sisters believed she was too young to serve as mother superior. When the provincial saw that she would lose the election he suspended the process and installed another nun as interim abbess. Some of the nuns, infuriated by this high-handed action, marched through the streets of Trujillo to the residence of the bishop, who listened to their complaints and then conferred with the provincial, who set the date for another election. As the day for the voting approached the city began to seethe with unrest, so the *corregidor* had the convent surrounded with soldiers, an act which insulted the nuns. When the time came to vote, twenty of the rebellious sisters refused to enter the capitular chamber; instead they demanded that the bishop be present during the casting of votes. The matter was finally resolved by the Audiencia, which decreed that both the provincial and the bishop should oversee the voting. The former aspirants to the office withdrew their names and another sister was elected. Mother Casanova died many years later, after having served as mother superior many times. We can be sure that the incongruity of seeing the brides of Christ wrangling over matters such as elections must have delighted Palma, who enjoyed pointing out human idiosyncrasies and failings where we do not expect to find them.

Of a different nature was the election of the patron saint of the Royal and Pontifical University of Lima, which in 1574 had just received its charter, signed by the king and the pope. Partisanship permeated the whole process; the rector and the other lawyers supported Saint Bernard, the medical faculty proposed Saint Cyprian, the theologians, Saint Thomas, the viceroy, Saint Augustine, and the

women, the four Evangelists. When the votes were counted no saint
received a majority, so another election was scheduled. The viceroy
withdrew the name of Saint Bernard and the women decided they
would pool their votes in favor of Saint Mark, but the second election,
which was bitterly contested, did not produce a clear majority. The
decision was then made to draw lots, so the names of the candidates
still in the running were put into the voting urn and a child drew out
the winner, which turned out to be the name of Saint Mark. Thus the
women of Lima were the victors even though they could not vote.
They coaxed, wheedled, and persuaded husbands, fathers, and their
gentleman friends until there were enough votes to make it possible
for their choice to be included in the drawing. This fascinating election
is treated in "El patronato de San Marcos" [The Patronage of San
Marcos], in which we see once again the truth of the saying "Never
underestimate the power of a woman." There is an ironic twist to this
story, for the university, which allowed no women to attend that
institution and which excluded women from teaching positions, was to
find itself bearing the name of a saint sponsored by women who
exerted sufficient pressure on their menfolk to have their way.

Other Additional Aspects of Religious Life in Peru

Fear of the Inquisition was ever present; therefore the "tradiciones"
are filled with the terrifying influence of that institution. However,
because Palma wrote a whole work on the Holy Office in his *Annals
of the Inquisition of Lima* the theme was used sparingly in his short
narrative pieces. One of the most interesting accounts deals with Juan
del Castellano, who was burned at the stake in 1608 because he
maintained that Adam had no navel. This piece, "El ombligo de
nuestro padre Adán" [Our Father Adam's Navel], also makes a point
of the fact that Castellano's father had been a Portuguese who was of
the Jewish faith. In 1639 eleven more Portuguese Jews met their
death in the flames of the Inquisition and fifty of their cobelievers
were punished by the Holy Office. In one piece, "Un reo de la
Inquisición" [A Criminal of the Inquisition], a pharmacist spent six
months in the cells of the Holy Office because his rival for the heart of
a young girl was an officer in that institution. When the officer, an old
man, lost out in the contest, he had the pharmacist imprisoned and

tortured on the charge that he refused to take off his cap and cross himself when the vesper bells were playing.

Ecclesiastics maintained that criminals, even murderers, had the right to seek refuge in churches. Since church buildings remained open and bells were rung on execution days there were occasions when those condemned to die escaped into churches to avoid punishment. An unusual story is that of Lieutenant Don Antonio de Erauzo, the nun-lieutenant who was really a woman disguised as a man. In a gambling fray she killed a Portuguese and was sentenced to death. But on the day of her execution (the authorities still thought she was a man) she snatched the Host from the priest hearing her confession and fled to the Church of Santa Clara. According to this "tradición," "¡A iglesia me llamo!" [I Seek Refuge in the Church!], she was safe, but in those days the hand of a person guilty of sacrilege for having touched the Host was to be scraped and passed through the flames. The criminal asked for confession and revealed her true identity, whereupon she was sent to Spain.

The ending of a similar episode in "Las querellas de Santo Toribio" [Santo Toribio's Disputes] is not so happy. When a murderer entered a church and claimed refuge there, the Viceroy ordered the alcalde to do his duty regardless of the necessity of having to disregard the privilege of refuge. Ignoring the protests of the clergy the alcalde removed the criminal from the church by force and placed him in prison. The archbishop threatened the alcalde with excommunication if he did not return the prisoner to the church. The alcalde showed his defiance of the archbishop by hanging the murderer and leaving his body swinging from the gallows. In this struggle between ecclesiastical and civil authority the Church was forced to give ground and the alcalde won out temporarily despite excommunication threats. But his triumph was shortlived because the next day the archbishop excommunicated him. Everyone shunned him and his constables resigned their positions. Finally, to cope with the situation he presented himself at the cathedral, where the archbishop administered three ritual strokes to his bare back and lifted the excommunication. That same day the alcalde resigned his position. In the previous "tradición" refuge in a church was considered lawful and the civil government respected it; in the one just treated the civil government did not recognize refuge in a church as lawful. It appears that circumstances altered cases and that in "Santo Toribio's Disputes" the right of refuge was not recognized by the alcalde because he didn't dare disobey the viceroy. Thus the legality of the seeking of refuge in a church did not seem to be at issue; it was rather a question of the power the viceroy was able to exert.

Palma enjoys writing about the role the Church played in Peru. He seems to be fascinated by the Inquisition and the great power the Church could apply in all facets of life. But his principal focus is on the Church as an institution which is beset with human frailties in spite of its high spiritual calling. He delights in pointing out cases of pride, hypocrisy, petulance, worldliness, and unwillingness to turn the other cheek. He marvels at the fear generated by the Inquisition and the threat of excommunication and satirizes the credulity and superstition which seemed to be fostered by some of the clergy. Perhaps his harshest attacks against the Church were leveled against its selling spiritual gifts and services for money. Surely, he seems to say, the Catholic Church should be more humanitarian, should strive more diligently to translate Christ's teachings into action.

The Viceroys

The first viceroy in Peru, Don Blasco Núñez de Vela, was appointed by Charles V and reigned from 1544 to 1546. The last viceroy, Don José de la Serna e Hinajosa, was number forty; he was appointed by Ferdinand VII and ruled from 1821 to 1824, when Peru won its independence. With the exception of the sixth viceroy, Don Martín Henríquez (1581–1583), all of the viceroys are presented to us in the "tradiciones," some as important characters and most of them in historical digressions. Palma's first portrayal of a viceroy is revealed in one of his primitive pieces, "Lida" (1853), in which he provides historical data about Don Diego Fernández de Córdova, Marquis of Guadalcázar (1622–1629), the thirteenth viceroy of Peru. Although Palma touched on the lives of several viceroys in the "tradiciones" penned in the next twenty years, it appears that he first conceived the idea of treating individual viceroys in the historical digression which became a hallmark of his Second Series in 1873, when he wrote "Las orejas del alcalde" [The Mayor's Ears]. But another ten years would pass before he would gather all of the "tradiciones" from the various series in which viceroys are prominent and place them in the Second Series (1883). Thus in one collection are found all of the "tradiciones" dealing with the viceroys. It had taken him exactly thirty years from the time that he had stumbled on this rich vein before he employed the format and conceived of the organization that would make the Second Series famous and stamp it as the collection of the viceroys.

The treatment of all thirty-nine viceroys is not feasible in this study; therefore four of the most outstanding viceroys will be considered. In passing, it should be noted that if Palma is a reliable judge of Peru's viceroys, the great majority of them were weak or incompetent or both.

His Excellency Don Melchor de Navarra y Rocafull, Duke of Palata, Prince of Masa, and Marquis of Tola, was the twenty-second viceroy of Peru and governed from 1681 to 1689. The Duke of Palata was a descendant of the royal family of Navarra and a member of the council that ruled Spain during the minority of Charles II. Of him Palma said that he was "el virrey más virrey que el Perú tuvo" ("he was the viceroy who was the most viceroy Peru has ever had"). His splendid entry into Lima was marked by royal pomp and by his walking on bars of silver when the cabildo received him. He established a royal court in miniature and rarely was he seen in the streets unless he was riding in a coach drawn by six horses which was magnificently escorted. No viceroy was more wise, industrious, just, energetic, and worthy of his position than he. When troublemakers sought to oppose him the Duke of Palata would say, "God is in His Heavens; the king is far away, and I rule here." An example of his firm rule is the setting aright of the Audiencias of Panama, Quito, Charcas, and Chile, putting a stop to their abuses, something which his predecessors had not done. During a period when pirate activity was a serious danger to the country, he took energetic steps to fight the buccaneers. First, he hanged every pirate then in jail; second, he fitted out flotillas which fought the buccaneers and forced them to retreat; and third, he built walls around Lima and Trujillo to repel pirate attacks. In 1684 he issued some orders placing some priests in a difficult position because of their exploitation of the Indians. The archbishop inveighed against Palata from the pulpit but the viceroy cut the ground out from under him by ordering tribunals and guilds not to take part in celebrations connected with the cathedral. Finally the archbishop swallowed his pride, but later he began to characterize the viceroy as an enemy of the Church, blaming him for the earthquakes suffered by Lima during this period. In 1689 the shocks caused a great deal of damage; of all the officers, only the viceroy kept his head and took positive steps in the midst of all the tribulation. The Duke of Palata was relieved of his duties in August of 1689, remained in Lima for a year, then died of yellow fever in 1690 while returning to Spain ("Cortar el revesino" [Cut the *Revesino*]). (This is a play in a card game called *revesino*.)

The year 1761 saw the arrival of his excellency Don Amat y Juniet, the thirty-first viceroy of Peru. Before ruling in that country he had been captain general in Chile, a training which other viceroys had experienced. He was a very active man, intelligent, an organizer, and just in the most rigorous sense. Very careful to defend the rights of the public, he was still able to defend his own. A very courageous man, he once put down an uprising of prisoners in Santiago when he entered the jail alone, and braving rocks thrown at him, held the rebels at bay with his sword. The next day he hanged eighteen of them. He effectively organized the defense of the western coast of Spanish America from Panama to Chile when an invasion from England was feared, sent arms and money to Paraguay and Buenos Aires, and organized a 7,000-man national guard in Lima. Very liberal in his religious views, he nevertheless exerted his influence toward forcing the friars to reform their way of life, which in many cases was not too holy. In order to spy on the friars Amat had a balcony built on the part of the palace that faced Desamparados Square. He spent many hours behind the blinds, keeping the activities of the monks under surveillance. Palma must have enjoyed very much showing the reader the highest officer in Peru, the representative of the Spanish monarch, spending hour after hour spying on the friars. This type of portrayal in which idiosyncrasies of important people are revealed in a comical manner was something in which the traditionist took pleasure.

Faced with an insurrection on the ships *Septentrión* and *Astuto* in the harbor of Callao, the viceroy flew the standard of justice from a tower, showed that he meant business with seven cannon shots, boarded the ships, and after a short investigation hanged ten of the ringleaders from the yardarm and had seventeen other mutineers shot. Amat always said that justice had to be like a bolt of lightning. He paid attention to the police force, the cleanliness, and the beauty of Lima. Facilities constructed during his term of office were a sailors' hospital, the Church of the Nazarenes, on which he worked as a carpenter, the Alameda, the Acho bullring, and the Coliseo, which was used for cockfights.

If his public record was a very praiseworthy one, his moral behavior scandalized the country. Involved in many love affairs, his relationship with a particular woman became one of the favorite topics in Lima. He fell head over heels in love with an actress, Micaela Villegas, whom he called Perricholi, and, in spite of his being harshly denounced by the women of the aristocracy, he allowed her to accompany him in public. Several "tradiciones" portray Perricholi; the most striking of them are "¡Pues bonita soy yo, la Castellanos!" [Well, I Am a Castellanos, and I Am a Beauty] and "Genialidades de la 'Perricholi' " ["Perricholi's" Idiosyncrasies]. According to one story she rode in a gilded coach to humiliate the aristocrats and then presented it to San Lázaro Church in order that the Blessed Sacraments might be carried to the dying more speedily. This is the same Perricholi who appears in Offenbach's opera *La Périchole,* Prosper Mérimée's play *Le Carrosse du Saint-Sacrement* [The Coach of the Holy Sacrament], and Thornton Wilder's novel *The Bridge of San Luis Rey.* Viceroy Amat was replaced in 1776, whereupon he returned to Spain and married a young niece in spite of being burdened down with some eighty years of age.

Another viceroy whose reign markedly benefited Peru was his excellency Don Teodoro de Croix, thirty-fourth viceroy of Peru, who made his entrance into Lima in 1784. Serving under his uncle, the Marquis of Croix, Viceroy of Mexico, he had spent many years in that country. Upon returning to Spain Charles III named him viceroy in Peru. According to one historian he was a man of eminent virtue who was recognized for his generosity, for on various occasions he stood with a candle in his hand, having given the silver candlestick holder to the poor because he lacked money to offer them. He was a devoted Christian who attended Mass regularly. This view of the Viceroy is presented in one of Palma's historical digressions in the "tradición" "La Gatita de Mari-Ramos que halaga con la cola y araña con las manos" ["Mari-Ramos, the Kitten that Flatters with Its Tail and Scratches with Its Paws"]. The author does not tell us how he reacts to de Croix's behavior, but if we read between the lines we can be sure that Palma enjoyed pointing to the human side of powerful figures. In this "tradición" Palma relates an anecdote in which de Croix plays an important role. The viceroy insisted on having four soft-boiled eggs for his noon meal and assigned his majordomo, Julian de Córdova, the task of selecting and buying them. Córdova carried out his responsibility very diligently, taking with him a ring and scales, for the eggs had to be large enough so they would barely pass through the ring and be of a certain weight. His meticulous ways of choosing eggs exasperated the store owners, but to add to their ill feelings, the majordomo constantly haggled over the price of the eggs. Finally the store owners in the vicinity agreed not to sell him any more eggs, whereupon Córdova had to go farther and farther to obtain eggs for the viceroy. When the majordomo asked for eggs the owners would always say, "We don't have any, Don Julian. You will have to go to the next corner for them." The situation became so bad that the majordomo could not buy any eggs within eight blocks of the palace. Before long the plight of the majordomo reached the ears of the viceroy, who said to Córdova one day, "Julian, where did you buy the eggs today?" The response was, "The corner of San Andrés." Whereupon Marquis de Croix said, "Well, tomorrow you will have to go to some other corner for them." "You are certainly right," replied the majordomo, "and the day will come when I will have to go to Jetafe to get them." (Jetafe, or Getafe, is a town situated a few miles from Madrid.) This series of events represents the origin of a children's game played in Lima during Palma's day called "huevos" ("eggs").

Although the Viceroy's social circle included some of Peru's most highly educated citizens, he gave orders forbidding the entrance of the works of the French encyclopedists into Peru. And in spite of the fact that he enjoyed reading the works of a caustic, libertine poet, he considered it to be an affront to his office when a priest asked him to read some of his own verses which were critical of the behavior of Spaniards in America. To show his displeasure and to teach other poets a lesson he exiled the unfortunate man to Spain. Palma doesn't comment further on this action by the viceroy.

"The English Viceroy," Don Ambrosio de O'Higgins, Marquis of Osorno, thirty-sixth viceroy of Peru, began his term of office in 1796. Born in Ireland of parents who were poor laborers, he spent the first years of his life carrying firewood to the kitchen of Dungan Castle, residence of Countess Bective. His uncle, a Jesuit priest in a monastery in Cádiz, brought him to Spain, gave him an education of sorts, and sent him to America with a *pacotilla* (goods carried by seamen free of freight charges) because he had shown an interest in commerce. At the age of twenty he was in Lima selling ribbons, needles, and thimbles ("A la cárcel todo Cristo" [To Jail, Everyone!]). The Irishman, nicknamed "Ambrose the Englishman," and a Spaniard nicknamed "Johnny the Mountaineer" were both peddlers who were well known in Lima during the 1760s. It wasn't long before the competition between them became very intense, and finally reached the point that they were stealing each other's goods. After two years of this bitter rivalry they realized that if the hostile actions continued they would both be ruined, so they decided to forget their past differences and become partners. Thus the former enemies began to live together and actually became the best of friends. Their business began to prosper and within a year they had turned a substantial profit. But before long they became too ambitious and too free with their money as they attempted to climb the social ladder with the result that they lost all that they had and found themselves deeply in debt. At this point the following conversation took place. "What do we do now?" asked the Spaniard. "What do we do? We turn the keys over to the authorities," said the Irishman. "What do you mean, the authorities? That's a lot of rubbish!" exclaimed his partner. "Let's close up the shop, throw the keys into the river and get out of here fast. Who knows what fate God has in store for us!" "At the very least," replied Ambrose, "an archbishop's miter for you and a viceroy's staff for me." "And why not?" asked the Spaniard. "Of much less God made a viceroy of Cañete." (The Marquis of Cañete, Viceroy Andrés Hurtado de Mendoza, ruled in Peru from 1556 to 1561.) The next day Ambrose and Johnny disappeared from Lima (Aguilar, p. 757).

The sixth of June, 1796, was a day of solemn celebration for the capital city. On that day the thirty-sixth viceroy, Don Ambrosio O'Higgins, Marquis of Osorno, made his triumphal entry into Lima. As soon as the cathedral bells announced that the new viceroy had entered the palace the archbishop, Juan Domingo González de la Reguera, entered his carriage and was driven to the viceroy's palace in order to make a visit required by etiquette. When the viceroy saw the archbishop he descended from his throne and the two embraced. In a low voice the following conversation took place. "Johnny! Who would have thought. . . !" "Ambrose! I told you so. . . . Of much less God made a viceroy of Cañete." Thus ends the "tradición," with no further comment from the author. It was this same Don Ambrosio O'Higgins who spent a night in jail as noted in the section dealing with nobility and honor. He died in 1800 and was buried in the vault of St. Peter's Church in Lima. ("De menos hizo Dios a Cañete" [Of Much Less God Made a Viceroy of Cañete]).

Miscellaneous Themes

Family and Home in Peru

Palma informs us in "El baile de la Victoria" [The Victory Ball] that the victory of the revolutionaries at the battle of Ayacucho did not bring about a sudden end to the colonial way of life. In fact the furniture, the clothing, religious holidays, bullfights, and theatrical performances remained the same for many years after Peru gained its independence. Even though the law prohibited the use of titles of nobility it was not uncommon to hear expressions such as: "Good health to you, Sir Marquis!" or "Goodbye, Sir Count!" With a satirical touch Palma suggests that those who used such titles did so because it was very pleasing to them to hear in return: "May God be with you, my Colonel!" or "Good luck to you, my General!" While Palma was growing up he came in contact with many former nobles who dressed with all of the ostentation and magnificence of the colonial period. But he was not impressed with their talents or their learning. In fact, he says, there were some who were so stupid that they hid bags of gold under their beds because they did not dare invest their money in business enterprises. One of the customs that Palma witnessed while a boy was something known as "vareando la plata," which consisted of throwing pieces of silver onto a blanket and beating them with a club so that the silver would not oxidize. Of such people Palma says that they and not the silver deserved the beating. Some would say of them: "That gentleman is a good man." In Palma's opinion there wasn't anything in Lima that was in greater abundance than good men who weren't good for anything.

In the same "tradición" we learn that every respectable home was run on the following schedule. From nine to ten in the morning, breakfast; from three to four in the afternoon, lunch or afternoon meal; at ten, dinner; and just before retiring, the saying of the Rosary. (In another piece, "El divorcio de la condesita" [The Divorce of the Little Countess], the hour for the saying of the Rosary was eight o'clock at night.) In the old days the women of Lima did not have a dress made every two weeks; they possessed four to six dresses made of Manila velvet which was expensive but of solid quality. Of these dresses one had been bequeathed to the owner by means of a will. And everyone had dishes made of silver. Only the destitute would think of eating from porcelain or earthenware dishes. Of course the food was more substantial than in 1910 when Palma wrote the piece. As he put it, those foods stuck to the ribs, unlike the French cuisine of his day, which, as he put it, was so much light sponge cake and worthless stuff. It is evident that Palma felt that in many ways life in the colonial period had marked advantages over the life he knew in the early part of the twentieth century.

The girls in even the finest families received very little education. They learned to read well enough to read about the saint of the day and learned to write well enough to put down instructions concerning the laundry. They played the harp, not always with great skill, repeated hymns to the Holy Trinity, and said their novenas. Other training they received included cooking, sewing, elementary arithmetic, and the Catechism. Carefully kept away from most men, young or old, girls were allowed to stay in the same room with elderly men who were friends of the family and priests who regularly heard their confessions. When a young man visited the home the young ladies were banished from the parlor, but this did not stop them from spying on the young fellow through the keyhole when the mothers' backs were turned. It is true that male cousins, considered by most to be neuter in gender, could talk with the girl, but conversing with other young men informally was out of the question. Of course there were times when these cousins who were thought to be incapable of any indiscretions obtained some of the forbidden fruit or caused other little scandals. Palma treats this topic with his usual humorous style, and although he says nothing directly to indicate how he feels about the way girls were treated the reader can be reasonably certain that he believed that they deserved a better education and that keeping them away from men in such a tyrannical fashion was unnatural and unwise ("The Divorce of the Little Countess").

Palma says very little about marriage in Peru, but he does provide information about the marriage bed and a strange way in which pregnant women insisted that their whims be indulged. The marriage bed of old Peru as presented in "La cama matrimonial" [The Matrimonial Bed] was always found in one of the largest rooms of the home and was placed on a hardwood platform raised a foot and a half from the floor. It was luxurious in its ornamentation and its curtains and was enclosed with a railing. In Palma's day such beds had disappeared and in their place were to be found twin beds and even beds in different rooms. One strange accessory used in the past was the *tablilla divisoria*, a piece of wood as long as the bed and one and one-half inches high, which divided the bed into two equal sections. According to the author, the confessor of each married couple imposed strict chastity on them during Holy Thursday and Good Friday and in order to eliminate the contact of bodies and thus reduce the temptation of sexual sin, the *tablilla* was placed in the bed. It appears likely that at times wives installed them temporarily when they were angry with their husbands or when they felt it best to enforce separation. But as Palma points out, most of the time the *tablilla* could be found in the room where junk accumulated. He seems to regret the passing of the patriarchal order in Peruvian homes and the disappearance of the marriage bed when he writes that in the past one of the joys of life was to have the mother and father assaulted in their bed by all their children, who would greet their parents with a "Good morning, daddy!" and a "Good morning, mommy!"

The woman who found herself pregnant in old Peru could satisfy her most extravagant caprices because the idea was prevalent that to deny her what she asked for would have a harmful effect on her unborn child ("La niña del antojo" [A Girl's Whim]). Even physicians subscribed to this notion, according to medical theses located in the National Library. Because visiting religious houses was forbidden, some pregnant women took it into their heads to demand permission to visit monasteries and convents of priests and nuns. Strangely enough, the ecclesiastical authorities, fearing that women in such a delicate condition might suffer a miscarriage or some other adversity if the request were not granted, authorized such visits. Thus the custom developed which made it possible for pregnant women to visit all the convents they desired to see. As soon as it was determined that a woman was with child she made plans with her sisters, friends, relatives, and maids to spend at least a month visiting one convent after another. While they were in the cloisters they were provided with a guide, shown every room they desired to see, and given flowers, fruit, religious objects, and other gifts upon their departure. Needless to say there were some abuses, such as women who were not pregnant but had filled out their stomachs with rags hidden under their skirts. On an unspecified date a certain archbishop required that before permission could be granted legal documents had to be prepared by the local authorities. His successor put an end to the custom by refusing once and for all to grant permission to visit cloisters. And thus came to an end one of the most fascinating practices in colonial Peru.

Matters which deal almost exclusively with women are portrayed by Palma with obvious relish in several "tradiciones." In these pieces we find information about care of the teeth and of the hair, about stockings, farthingales (hoop skirts, etc.), and the *saya y manto* (a particular kind of skirt and mantle). According to "La trenza de sus cabellos" [The Braid of Her Hair] Lima women did not use toothpaste or toothpowder; nevertheless, their teeth were always clean and regularly shaped because they chewed certain roots and scrubbed them against their teeth. These white and juicy roots were sold by peddlers. Since there were no hairdressers for the average woman, care of the hair was very simple. She used no curling irons, no papers, and no liquid hair preparation of any kind. She used water and nothing else. The adorning of hair with flowers was widespread and divided women into the married and the unmarried. The married woman placed the flowers on the right side of the head and the unmarried woman placed hers on the left side. Flowers were purchased from the *jazminero*, a peddler who appeared every afternoon; included among the most popular were jasmines, Arabian jasmines, *aromas* (acacia flowers), *suches* (tropical flowers related to dogbane), orange blossoms, and the cherimoya. Apparently flowers were chosen for their perfume and their beauty.

The importance of stockings for the women of Lima is seen in "Carencia de medias y abundancia de medios" [Scarcity of Stockings and Abundance of Means]. Because of the possibility of the breaking out of hostilities between Spain and England in 1788, no ships from the mother country arrived in Peru for a period of more than a year. Finally the *Santa Rufina*, out of Cádiz, arrived with a sizable stock of merchandise, among which was a shipment of two crates containing 240 pairs of stockings. Such an item would be in great demand, but they could not be sold because the customs officers insisted that they had not been manufactured in Spain and thus were contraband. The merchant to whom the stockings had been consigned protested the decision and was successful in having two reputable merchants swear under oath that the stockings were not contraband. Faced with a difficult situation the viceroy ordered that the two crates be placed in the customs house and that samples be sent to Spain in order that Charles III might hand down a decision. Ten months passed and the *limeñas* ("women of Lima") were becoming more unhappy and frustrated. At this point let us permit Palma to describe what happened:

Ten months went by. . .and the *limeñas* were careless in everything they did. They didn't go to dances nor did they go visiting, nor to processions, nor to the theater because they couldn't be seen with darned stockings or ones with holes in them.

In spite of all the efforts made to persuade the viceroy to release the stockings he stubbornly refused. The *limeñas* openly rebelled against the men, who [in their opinion] were a bunch of blockheads; after all they put up with a ruler who was on such unfriendly terms with the fair sex and they didn't even revolt against him.

There certainly was sufficient justification for hanging his Excellency!

Depriving the *limeñas* of an article of such vital importance! At the very least [in our day] we would have a ministerial crisis! It is very clear. Since the viceroy was not a married man nor a woman chaser he didn't understand anything about female needs. (Aguilar, p. 732)

But the narrative has a happy ending. Feelings were running high when the merchants, fearing that the women would not be satisfied with a war of words and that the situation might turn into a violent one, proposed that the stockings be sold under the condition that a deposit of 10,000 pesos be placed in the Royal Treasury until the decision should arrive from Spain. And thus the conflict came to an end long before the decision arrived which ruled against the customs officers.

In "Motín de limeñas" [Revolt of the Women of Lima] we read of an uprising which was narrowly averted in 1601 when the Audiencia in Peru wisely decided to ignore an edict handed down by Phillip III which made it unlawful for women to wear hoop skirts or to wear blouses with deep plunging necklines unless they were prostitutes. The punishment for disobeying the law was the loss of the hoop skirt or blouse and a fine of 20,000 *maravedís*. The edict had arrived from Spain on February 9, 1601, and the next day Lima was seething. A large mass of humanity had congregated on the steps of the still-to-be-completed cathedral and was milling around in a very agitated manner. In the courtyard of the viceroy's palace a company of lancers, the personal escort of the chief officer of Peru, was at the ready. With them was a regiment of infantry carrying muskets and artillery men ready to fire four mortars. The situation was tense indeed, and it had arisen because of the king's order. Priests and town council members went among the women trying to calm them down. This is the situation as Palma describes it:

"[What we need is] good judgment, good judgment; don't throw yourselves into a lion's den!" shouted Antonio Pesquera, a friar who was so chubby that he seemed to be about ready to have a heart attack. He was the prelate of the Mercedarians, who had been in Lima since the days of Pizarro. . . . "Calm down," said Don Damián Salazar, councilman in charge of sales tax collections, as he moved among the women in another group, "everything doesn't have to end up in violence." "There is no need to get upset," another councilman harangued them. "Everything will turn out the way you want it, according to what I have just heard the viceroy say. Let's wait. Let's wait a little while." Whereupon a young girl who was wearing a carnelian ornamental comb and *aromas* and jasmines in her curled hair murmured:

> Many live happily
> with their hopes;
> many are the donkeys
> that eat green [grass]. (Aguilar, p.234)

Finally the priests and town council members were able to pacify the women by reporting to them that the Audiencia would discuss the matter. The decision of that body was that the edict should be left as an *hostia sin consagrar,* which means that the order was legal, but that it would not become law in Peru. Sometimes the viceroy dramatized noncompliance with an edict by kissing the paper on which it was written, holding it even with his head and saying with a loud voice, "Acato y no cumplo" ("I respect it but I will not obey it"). The day ended on a happy note as the jubilant women celebrated their triumph with elegant balls, fireworks, and other activities. Palma's attitude was certainly one of cheering the women on, even though he doesn't make any direct statements concerning his views on the matter. However, in the next "tradición" we will see that at times he expressed his ideas about such matters with clarity.

Serious enough were these conflicts involving stockings and hoop skirts, but they pale into insignificance when compared with the uproar which developed when the viceroy prohibited the wearing of the *saya y manto* in 1601. ("La tradición de la saya y manto" [The Tradition of the *Saya y Manto*]). During this period the *saya* was a skirt which was like a sheath from the waist to the feet and restricted movement so much that the longest step that could be taken measured just three inches. The *manto* was a mantle which was wrapped around the shoulders and the head in such a fashion that only one eye was left uncovered, which provided a very effective way of hiding one's identity. Palma notes that it was impossible to distinguish between women wearing this apparel because they looked so much alike that their husbands and even their fathers were unable to recognize them.

The *saya y manto* were especially popular with women in Lima because they could flirt and otherwise bedevil men without revealing their identity. Palma hazards the guess that their use developed in 1560 and points out that these particular garments were not known in Spain; in fact they were worn in just one Peruvian city—Lima. In spite of various attempts to eliminate them they continued to be popular until about 1850, at which time French styles became fashionable. By 1860 the *saya y manto* had completely disappeared. Several viceroys and an archbishop tried to prohibit their use because of the immorality they gave rise to, but to no avail.

The most serious confrontation occurred in 1601 when Archbishop Toribio de Mogrovejo proposed to the Third Council that the wearing of the *saya y manto* to religious services or to processions be prohibited under pain of excommunication. The matter was discussed in secret session but soon everyone in Lima knew what was being proposed, and all the women were considerably upset. The casting of votes was scheduled for the following day and during the intervening twenty-four hours the *limeñas,* led by the wife of the viceroy, Doña Teresa de Castro, conspired to have the proposition defeated, but not through protests or petitions. The details of what the *limeñas* did are found in another "tradición" entitled "La conspiración de la saya y manto" [The Conspiracy of the *Saya y Manto*]. They merely refused to take care of their homes and families. They didn't clean their homes, cook decent meals, take proper care of their children, wash the clothes, or mend their husbands' stockings. They neglected everything in their conspiratorial zeal. The archbishop, realizing that the cause was lost, postponed the casting of votes and before the matter could be resolved the council was dissolved, due in great part, in Palma's opinion, to the fact that the women conspired against its existence. Palma makes the following comment about the attempt to legislate in matters concerning the clothes women should wear: "The viceroys, the Marquis Guadalcázar and Montesclaros, and others tried to abolish the *saya y manto* but to no avail. There was one viceroy who was content to recommend to the husbands that they not allow wife [*costilla*—which means rib] or daughters to wear such clothing, which was tantamount to making a recommendation to the Archipámpano of the Indies [a person of imaginary rank or office]. So certain is it that we men take no part in [female] fashions that even today we do nothing about them when [our women] sport those phenomenally huge hats that are all the rage. They will disappear without our intervention" (Aguilar, p. 161). In another remark about the futility of trying to pass laws dealing with fashions Palma wrote: "It is superfluous to say that the *limeñas* held their banner high and that the viceroys were always routed. In order to legislate concerning feminine matters one has to have more courage than to storm the barricades. It is true also that we, those of the ugly sex, deep down inside, backed up the *limeñas* any way we could, encouraging them to make hair curler papers and paper cones of the paper on which were printed the calamitous decrees" (Aguilar, p. 165).

Peddlers in Lima

Palma decries the elimination of the poeticized Peru that was part of the colonial tradition. With independence and progress came a tendency to make life more prosaic because some of the more picturesque customs and practices fell into disuse. One aspect of life in Lima that he was sorry to see disappear was the regularity with which peddlers would appear at a particular location and announce their wares. According to Palma they were so punctual in their arrival that one could set his watch according to the following schedule:

6:00 A.M.—the milk vendor (female)

7:00 A.M.—the tea vendor and the *chicha* vendor (*chicha*—a kind of beer)

8:00 A.M.—the biscuit or cake vendor and the pot vendor

9:00 A.M.—the vendor of *zanguito de ñajú* (sweet made of corn flour and mallow)

10:00 A.M.—the tamale vendor

11:00 A.M.—the melon vendor

12:00 P.M.—the fruit vendor

1:00 P.M.—the vendor of *ante con ante* (beverage made from fruit, sugar, cinnamon, and nutmeg); the rice and *alfajor* vendors (*alfajor*— candy made of yucca flour, ginger, cane syrup, and nuts)

2:00 P.M.—the doughnut vendor, the vendor of *humita* (dish made from corn, hot peppers, tomatoes, grease, and sugar)

3:00 P.M.—the vendor of molasses candy, the vendor of nougats, and the vendor of *anticucho* (small pieces of beef on a stick)

4:00 P.M.—the vendor of highly seasoned fried foods and the vendor of *piñita de nuez* (possibly a type of pine nut candy)

5:00 P.M.—the vendor of fresh flowers and the vendor of cloth flowers

6:00 P.M.—the vendor of roots and the vendor of sweetbreads

7:00 P.M.—the vendor of caramels and the vendor of *mazamorra* (type of thick corn soup)

8:00 P.M.—the vendor of ices and the vendor of waffles

9:00 P.M.—although not a peddler, the *animero* (parish sacristan) made his rounds at this hour, which was also the hour of curfew. He solicited contributions for souls in Purgatory or for wax for Our Lord.

10:00 P.M.—From this time on the *sereno* or night watchman would announce each hour, saying something like this, "¡Ave María Purísima! Ten o'clock! Long live Peru; all is well!"

This information is found in "Con días y ollas venceremos" [With Days and Jars We Will Conquer]. In the same piece Palma expresses his feelings about life in those days: "Oh, such happy times! Someone might try to show off out of pure ostentation by flashing his watch, but in order to know what time it really was there was nothing more punctual than the calls of the vendors. That system was so accurate that it was always correct to the second and it didn't have to be cleaned, either, or sent to the hospital [watchmaker's shop] every six months. And then there is the cheapness! Well, when I start to talk about customs of the past I forget what I'm doing and my pen gallops along like a runaway horse" (Aguilar, p. 961).

Although not included in the preceding schedule the *aguadores* or water carriers receive special attention from Palma, as we see in "Los aguadores de Lima" [The Water Carriers of Lima]. When Pizarro founded Lima each family had to assign a servant to bring water from the river in earthen jars, but when black slaves were bought by wealthy families they were sent to the neighboring hills for water, which they brought back in two casks on a donkey. In 1650 a fountain was constructed in the Plaza Mayor and a guild of water carriers was organized. It was composed of fifteen or twenty blacks who delivered two casks of water for half a silver *real*. From the very first the *aguadores* were known for their scurrilous language, to the extent that mothers would reprove their children saying, "Be quiet, children! Your language sounds like that of the *aguadores*." Their charter included the following duties. Every Saturday, from four to five, they were to water the principal squares, including the Plaza Mayor, Merced Square, and San Agustín Square. One afternoon every two weeks they were required to reduce the canine population by killing every dog found in the streets not wearing a collar obtained by the owner from the police for two pesos. The *aguadores* would arm themselves with clubs tipped with lead and beat and smash the unfortunate animals until the streets of Lima looked like a slaughter-house. Horrible indeed were the afternoons set aside for the reduction of the canine population. This practice continued until 1856 or 1857, when poisoned meat was set out by the water carriers. The use of poison made it necessary that the afternoon of the *bocadillo* ("snack") all dogs be kept off the streets because the poisoned meat killed all dogs, whether they were homeless curs or the property of wealthy families. When the guild ceased to function dogs were allowed to roam at will in Lima.

With the arrival of the republic the *aguadores* were given an added responsibility, that of carrying out the government's will during elections. A certain well-to-do gentleman by the name of Don José Francisco felt that he could control the political situation in Lima if he could control the guild, which he proceeded to do by befriending the members of the guild whenever they found themselves in trouble with the law. He became so intimately associated with the guild that when meetings were held in the Plaza Mayor to lay plans for future activities, Don José was there and would answer the roll just like any other member. While elections were being held all of the water carriers would meet together in some old home, where they would eat, drink, and carouse until Don José would appear, gun in hand, and tell them to go to a particular voting place where government candidates were losing and remedy the situation. Armed with daggers and clubs, the two hundred *aguadores* would fall upon the unsuspecting voters and voting authorities, smash a few heads, and put the rest to flight. Thus the opposition lost its advantage and the government was able to manipulate the elections as it wished. When the guild of water carriers ceased to exist one more of Lima's fascinating traditions died out. As Palma finished the "tradición" he wrote: "Thanks be to God, for almost forty years now elections have been held without any blood-shed. Some elections have been characterized by peaceful tricks and confusion, which have replaced the democratic cudgel of the water carriers, a guild which now is nothing more than one of so many memories of the traditions of the past" (Aguilar, p. 393).

Physicians and Quack Doctors

Indicative of Palma's opinion of the medical profession during the colonial period is the fact that he referred to them as *matasanos* (literally, killers of the healthy). This attitude can also be found in one of Palma's compatriots, Juan del Valle Caviedes, a seventeenth-century poet who is remembered principally for his scathing denuncia-tions of Lima's physicians. In the opinion of Valle Caviedes they were all incompetent and some of them almost killed him when he became ill. His works had circulated in unpublished form until 1873, when Manuel Odriozola, at the time director of the National Library, published an edition of his poetry in the *Documentos literarios del Perú* and Palma wrote a prologue for it which was later included in his "tradiciones" ("El poeta de la Ribera don Juan del Valle y Caviedes" [The Poet of the River Bank Don Juan del Valle y Caviedes]).

According to "El latín de una limeña," one of the reasons doctors were so unpopular was that they used Latin so much that most people did not know what they were saying. If they had to die they preferred to die listening to their own language. In reality, in Palma's jesting opinion, the Latin the doctors spoke (and it was probably poor Latin) sent more patients to their death than the remedies they prescribed. As a result of this dislike for pedantic, Latin-speaking doctors, home remedies and special blessings for the sick were popular. For a sunstroke, nothing was better than a prayer in honor of the Virgin Mary; to induce sweating, the Creed; the best poultices were the Gospels, applied directly to the stomach. *Jaculatorias* (short, sudden prayers) were effective against the seven-day sickness, and small glass balls were used by some friars to prevent emaciation of children or to defend them against witches who would suck the life from them. In the seventeenth century a great many physicians believed that astrology was an integral part of medical practice, according to "La astrología

en el Perú" [Astrology in Peru]. Certain diseases flourished when
particular planets entered certain houses. For example, when the sun
was in the house of Aries tuberculosis was to be feared and when the
sun was in the house of Virgo stomach tumors were dangerous.
According to these physicians there were even astrological situations
during which any slight illness would lead inexorably to the grave. For
the information concerning astrology and medicine Palma resorted to
a book of 700 pages by Juan de Figueroa, familiar of the Holy Office.
It was published in Lima in 1660 and was entitled *La astrología en la
medicina* [Astrology in Medicine]. With respect to the popularity of
the work Palma states: "There is no desire on my part to cover a lot of
pages with writing, for with what I have noted here there is sufficient
for the reader to get a good idea concerning the book, which enjoyed
great popularity in its time. There was not a well-governed household
or a harmonious married couple which didn't have a copy [of the
work] which was handled more than *La alfalfa espiritual para los
borregos de Cristo* [Spiritual Alfalfa for Christ's Lambs] or the bull of
the Crusades."

A *curandera* (female quack) appears in a "tradición" told in the
style of tía Catita entited "La misa negra." This is the way the
"tradicionista" introduces the protagonist, Ña San Diego.

Once upon a time. Air for birds, water for fishes, fire for the wicked, the
earth for the righteous and glory for the very best; and you are the very best,
little angels of my choir; may His Divine Majesty make saints of all of you
without vigils.

Well, little children, in 1802, Avilés reigned, a viceroy who was as good
as a hot biscuit. It was then that I became acquainted with Mother San
Diego. Many times I saw her in the nine o'clock mass in Santo Domingo
church, and it was a delight to see her so contrite and to see her so transported
in ecstasy that she didn't touch the ground until she reached the communion
rail. I considered her blessed, but later on you will see that all of this was
nothing more than the cunning, the deceit and the confusion of the Devil.
Cross yourselves, children, to frighten off that evil creature.

At that time Ña San Diego was about fifty years old and she went from
house to house healing the sick, for which kindnesses she received some alms.
She didn't use remedies from the pharmacy but relics and prayers and by
placing the belt of her garment on the pit of the stomach . . . she could cure

the most rebellious upset stomach. She cured a toothache that I had by praying mentally [silently] for an hour and applying to my face a bone that had belonged to Saint Faustus, Saint Saturnine, Saint Theophilus, Saint Julian, Saint Acriano or Saint Sebastian; the Pope had sent a whole load of the bones of those saints to the Cathedral of Lima. When you get older you can ask the archbishop or Canon Cockroach; they will tell you that I am not lying. So it wasn't the zealous churchgoer who cured me, but the Devil, may God forgive me, for if I sinned it was out of ignorance. Make the sign of the cross and don't squeeze your fingers together, and cross yourselves again, little angels of the Lord. (Aguilar, p. 833)

Subsequent events proved, according to Catita, that this quack was a witch because testimony was given that she cohabited with the Devil. (At this point in the narrative tía Catita realizes that such talk may not be appropriate for the ears of her young listeners. Palma thus portrays the situation this way: "Then this San Diego woman declared that for ten years she had been living [Jesus, Mary and Joseph!] in concubinage with Old Nick. You don't know what concubinage is, and may the good Lord grant that you never find out. To make amends for my lack of discretion and for having allowed that wicked word to escape from my lips you must recite the Creed with your arms extended [in the form of a cross]"). On August 27, 1803, after having been examined by the Inquisition, she was sentenced to ride a donkey to the church of Santo Domingo wearing a *coroza* (conical hat made of paper) and a sanbenito. From there she was taken to a house for lay sisters, where she died before Peru won its independence.

One barbarous practice was carried out by *despenadores*, who would put to death a sick person who was thought to be beyond help. In "Fray Juan Sin Miedo" [Friar John Fearless] we learn that in the colonial period there was a type of mercy killing which made it possible for certain individuals to exercise the macabre vocation of putting dying individuals out of their misery. When the *curandero* pronounced the patient to be moribund the relatives called in a *despenador* to cut short his suffering. The mercy killer was usually an Indian of ugly, sinister mien who lived apart from everyone else. Having received his pay, two to four pesos, he would sit on the chest of the patient, grasp the head, force his very large finger nail into the depression of the throat and strangle him quickly and efficiently. This information appears as a digression in the "tradición" cited and Palma's only personal comment on the grisly practice is the following: "The last *despenador* died fifty years ago in Huacho, thanks be to God, and the custom died out forever."

Although physicians made good use of quinine, it was not discovered originally by doctors or even by scientists. "Los polvos de la condesa" [The Powders of the Countess] reveals that the marvelous powers of the drug were discovered by an Indian in Peru quite by accident. Afflicted with malaria he drank from the backwater of a certain river and was healed because some cinchona trees were growing on the banks of the river. Later he saved the lives of others by having them drink water in which he had infused roots from the tree. The Indian revealed his secret to a Jesuit priest, who healed the viceroy's wife, the Countess of Chinchón, in 1631. For many years the Jesuits alone knew about the drug; for this reason it was known as "the powder of the Jesuits." An English physician, Mr. Talbot, cured some important Frenchmen, including the Prince of Condé, the Dauphin, and Colbert, using quinine; later he sold the knowledge of the drug to the French government for a sizable sum of money and a pension for life. Linnaeus gave it the scientific name of Cinchona because of the role played in the discovery by the Countess of Chinchón. At first the use of quinine in Europe met serious opposition. In Salamanca it was held that any doctor prescribing it was in mortal sin because the powers it possessed could be attributed to a pact made by Peruvians with the Devil.

Barbers

One of Palma's most engaging pieces is "¡Feliz barbero!" [Happy Barber!], a "tradición" in which many of the duties of a barber are outlined. The setting for the narrative is Huánuco, a city in which the blue-blooded aristocracy, who were descendants of conquistadores, felt they were superior to everyone else. In fact they thought they had been formed of a different kind of clay and came very close to saying, like the conceited Portuguese, that they didn't descend from Noah, for when that drunkard was saved from the flood in his ark, they (the Braganzas) were saved also, but in their own small boat. The protagonist of the story is Don Fermín García Gorrochano, who, says Palma, was more noble of course than the Cid and the Seven Infantes of Lara. At this point let us permit Palma's pen to describe what happened.

Don Fermín was what one could call a dandy who was very stuck on himself and who continually boasted of his blue blood. Wealthy and noble he thought only of amorous adventures and it appears that he was as successful in them as Caesar and Alexander were in other kinds of conquests.

One particular day his thoughts were centered on a rendezvous which was to take place during the hours when our grandfathers used to take their siesta. It is not necessary to say that it was the kind of engagement to which he would not send an alter ego.

His servant had been trying to catch up with Higinio the barber since eight in the morning; anyone who wants to harvest the first leaves of the vine, the myrtle and laurel in Venus's estate must present himself with his hair well trimmed and well groomed in every respect. Appearance counts for a great deal in matters of State and of the heart [*del Dios Cupido*].

But the accursed barber was busier that day than a treasury clerk in times of serious financial problems and business failures.

He had to apply leeches to a friar, mustard plasters to a young lady, extract the root of a tooth from the *corregidor*'s wife, shave a member of the town council, trim an acolyte's tonsure and cut off the braids of a girl who seemed to be headed in the wrong direction. When I say that there was a lot of hustle and bustle I really mean it!

"Tell his grace that as soon as I apply these cupping glasses to the priest's daughter I will take care of his needs," replied the barber to the entreaties of the servant.

"There is no mute barber nor wise singer" runs the saying.

Later on he said, "As soon as I shave the *fiel de fechos* [someone who functioned as a notary in a town where there wasn't one] and the inspector I will be with his grace.

The nobleman muttered, "And what do I do with this hair that has grown more than a poor man's money in the possession of a usurer?"

In such goings on and comings and goings, like in the children's game of *corregüela* [played with a stick and a looped strap] search for him inside and search for him outside, the three o'clock hour came and went and Don Fermín missed the date he had looked forward to with such anticipation. (Aguilar, p. 319)

When the barber finally arrived at the nobleman's home Don
Fermín was fit to be tied. Without saying a word to the poor fellow he
started to slap and kick him. Around the living room went the barber
with Don Fermín in hot pursuit until he saw an open door and tried to
escape through it. Unfortunately for him the door opened onto a
balcony and just as he left the room the nobleman gave him a mighty
kick that sent him sprawling into the street below. The fall killed him
instantly. As his body lay there a lady of the aristocracy came by,
looked at the corpse, and instead of fainting said, "What a fine death!
Such a lucky barber to die at the hands of a gentleman!" Palma's only
comment is: "Upon my faith! That is really heart-felt consolation—
say I." From this "tradición" we can see that barbers had many jobs
to perform, that sometimes they committed themselves too heavily and
made appointments they would be hard-pressed to keep. It also appears
that their lives were of little concern and that failing to keep an
appointment merited stern punishment.

Streets and Related Matters

The names of the streets of Lima constituted one of the clear
evidences that the town councils of Palma's day were divesting the city
of its historical memories and its poetical qualities. In a comment on
the street once known as "Mogollón" he said: "By that name we
knew it until there came along a prosaic town council which changed
the name, transforming the map of the city into a hodgepodge by
changing all the streetnames and waging a war to the death against
the poetic memories of a city which hides a story, a drama, a tradition
in every stone" ("Mogollón," [The Sponger]). The "tradición"
entitled "La faltriquera del Diablo" (The Devil's Pouch) contains an
entire section which deals with streets and their names. In one of the
paragraphs Palma complains about the changes that have taken place.

Before getting involved in the "tradición" I would like to set down the
origin of the names with which many of the streets of this republican and
formerly aristocratic city of the kings of Peru were baptized. In spite of the
fact that officially they have tried to change the names of these streets no
citizen of Lima pays any attention to them and, upon my faith, they are
absolutely right. For my part I can say that I never use the modern names:

first, because the past deserves some respect and there is nothing to be gained by abolishing names; and second, because such statutes by the authorities are so many scraps of paper [*papel mojado*] and with the passing of the years will serve only to cause us to forget what entered into our memories along with our primers. (Aguilar, pp. 398–99)

Palma informs us that when the city of Lima was first founded streets were named according to the most important individuals who lived on them. Thus names such as Azaña, Bravo, Mestas, Villegas, Zavala, and many others began to be used. Other streets received names connected with certain events, business activities, trees, saints, etc. For example, there was the street of the Marble of Carvajal, so named because a marble marker was placed on the site of the home of the traitor Francisco de Carbajal to make his name infamous forever. The street of the Blue Powder was the site of stores which sold anil, and the locations of the first slaughterhouses were dubbed the street of the Slaughterhouse of San Francisco and the street of the Slaughterhouse of San Jacinto.

During the colonial period the streets of Lima must have presented a very primitive picture. Most of them were not paved in any way and those that were paved were laid with rough cobblestones which were so uneven that a coach made a terrible racket when it bounced along through the thoroughfares of the capital of Peru. At night it must have been a frightening experience to walk the streets of the city. The majority of the streets were not lighted and must have been as black as pitch. Here and there a feeble candle flame of a votary candle in a niche set in a wall would flicker in an eerie way. Possible obstacles encountered on these streets without sidewalks were coaches, horses, mud puddles, and bandits. Of course there was the special danger of stumbling into the ditches which crisscrossed the city and served as sewers until pipes were laid in more enlightened times. Night or day their odor was disgusting and the sight of them was extremely repugnant. One detail which is worthy of mention is that it was common practice for the inhabitants to soak their wooden tubs in which they took their baths in these ditches so that the wood did not dry out and warp. One ostentatious gentleman soaked his tub every day, in spite of the fact that it was made of solid silver. He wanted to make sure that everyone knew that his bathtub was made of a precious metal, not of wood. The information for these details about street conditions is found in "Un virrey hereje y un campanero" [A Heretical Viceroy and a Bell Ringer] and "¡Ijurra! ¡No hay que apurar la burra!" [Ijurra! There Is No Need of Hurrying Up the Donkey!].

Superstitions

In an article entitled "Supersticiones de los peruanos" [Superstitions of the Peruvians] Palma berates the Catholic Church for its belief in laughable miracles and its reverence for images of saints. The Indians were very superstitious before the arrival of the white man, so the superstitions the Europeans brought with them fell on fertile soil. In the section dealing with the Catholic Church in Chapter 4 some material concerning superstitions has already been provided. One additional comment by Palma from the same article is appropriate. He made reference to a manuscript which contained information concerning superstitions. Although the author's name was not to be found in any part of the work, Palma believed that the Peruvian Don Juan Gastelú had written it. Of this manuscript Palma wrote:

Gastelú's manuscript abounds in anecdotes about criminal acts committed by priests, acts that if committed in advanced societies would cause the guilty person to be carried off to jail. We omit them because what has already been included is sufficient to give the reader a clear idea of the backwardness and the prevailing superstitions in a race that is far from being refractory to civilization and which, if schools were multiplied, would easily give up stupid errors and outlandish traditional customs. (Aguilar, p. 1434)

The following are superstitions that were commonly believed in Peru. The sight of many swallows was a sure sign of rain. A cricket in the home meant that the next day the owner would receive some money; a smarting or stinging of the palm of the hand meant the same thing. A locust signaled the arrival of a visitor. A snake crossing the path of a caravan foretold the death of someone in the caravan. When lice began to abandon the head and other parts of the body of a sick Indian he would die shortly thereafter. To dream of the extraction of a tooth or of the extinguishing of lights or the flooding of a river signified the death of a relative. To be pursued by a bull, a wild dog, or thieves was an augury of sickness. To make a woman fall in love with him an Indian would thread a needle and pass it through the eyes of a snake. He then carried the thread with him in his pocket. Others killed a lizard in December, reduced it to powder, then put some of it in beverages. Such a mixture, it was believed, would produce an erotic frenzy in any woman drinking it. Some guitars were made in such a way that playing them would cause a woman to fall in love with the man who was playing the instrument. Such a guitar was made with strings of snake nerves or tendons. One practice is particularly noteworthy because it shows the mixture of Indian and Christian customs. According to the manuscript perused by Palma a young Indian widow was taken by her relatives to a river where she was obliged to bathe in the nude in the presence of her kin. This ritual purified her and made her eligible to marry again. Another type of purification required that the widow engage in an orgy with three men, one representing God the Father, one Saint Peter and the third Saint Joseph. Palma's tongue-in-cheek comment about this latter practice is that after a woman is purified in this manner she will surely find a new husband. Certainly there is no question about how Palma feels about these superstitions, whether they be of Indian or European origin. In spite of the fact that they are very interesting they are evidences of a benighted culture which needs education and reason in order to eliminate practices and beliefs which at times may be harmless and laughable but in others may cause serious problems and even death. In Palma's view, "man is superstitious by nature. Everything that is fantastic and has in it the marvelous impresses and attracts him. There is no theogony without fables and miracles. Only by civilizing mankind, making it possible for reason to prevail over belief, can superstition be killed off" (Aguilar, p. 1430).

Unfortunately, the full impact of Palma's "tradiciones" cannot be fully appreciated after this brief view of some of the more prominent and interesting topics and themes, principally because it is impossible to convey an appreciation for the powerful role Palma's language played in these works. But in spite of this serious shortcoming the reader is able to become acquainted with a culture foreign to his own—one in which honor, the Catholic Church of yesteryear, and the viceroys occupy a conspicuous place. People and events are summoned from the limbo to which they had been relegated and play out their roles vigorously and colorfully. Thus they portray what was vital, picturesque, and significant in old Peru. Palma's rendering of that reality may suffer from inaccuracies and exaggerations, but his basic view of society in Peru remains after a century has passed by a revealing and penetrating portrayal of a great people. Would that every nation could count among its writers such a skillful and incisive interpreter.

Chapter Five

Lesser Works

The Poetry of Ricardo Palma

Ricardo Palma published six volumes of poetry in addition to many poems never published in any collection which appeared in newspapers, magazines and albums of lady friends. He wrote his first published poem in 1848, "A la memoria de la Sra. Da. Petronila Romero" [To the Memory of Doña Petronila Romero]. His last individual collection, "Filigranas" [Filigrees], was published in 1892 and in 1911 Palma published a volume entitled *Poesías completas* [Complete Poems], which contained most of the poetry he had published during his career.[1] If we compare his career as a poet with his career as a writer of "tradiciones" we note that they are parallel. He began writing verses about three years before he wrote his first extant prose piece and when he published *Complete Poems* he had written all but a few of his "tradiciones." Another parallel that is significant is that in his poetry and his prose Palma began as a Romantic. His Romanticism became very strong after he had been writing several years; then it began to weaken and in the same period of his life he rejected Romanticism in prose and poetry in a forthright manner. In his "tradiciones" this change has been documented in Chapter 2, where it was demonstrated that it took place shortly before the publication of the First Series, which was printed in 1872. We see this same change very clearly in his poetry when he published *Verbos y gerundios* [Verbs and Present Participles, 1877], in which we see no vestiges of the Romantic style which had been apparent in his preceding volume of poems, *Pasionarias* [Passionflowers, 1870], a collection which contains verses written between 1865–1870. A perusal of Palma's last "tradiciones" and his last three collections of poetry reveal, that the Romantic style is gone completely. However, in his "tradiciones" Palma is still very Romantic with respect to the historical setting and his desire to bury his life in the past. In his poetry he writes very little about the past, and colonial history, which he depicts so skillfully in prose, does not inspire any of his poems.

In addition to helping us see how Palma's attitude toward Romanticism changed, his poetry can shed some light on other facets of his life and career. Writes Alberto Tauro concerning the value of the study of Palma's early poetry: "[In this article we bring forth a rich selection of Ricardo Palma's juvenile poems] but we don't do it in the belief that we can add new value to his poetic vein, rather we find in them a documentation that is exceptional if we want to recognize the foundation and the projections of his aesthetic position and if we want to orient the biographer in the delineation of Palma's moral portrait."[2] Palma's poetry will be studied according to the following plan: the first division will cover poetry published from 1848 to 1860; the second, from 1860 to 1870, and the third, from 1870 to 1892. These periods correspond to his very early Romantic stage, his later Romantic stage, and the stage in which Romanticism disappears almost completely.

1848–1860

Palma's first poem, "To the Memory of Doña Petronila Romero," honors a woman whose influence on Palma's life has never been determined. Here is one strophe of the poem:

> ¿Por qué mi alma conmueve la campana
> Que toca ¡ay! con funeral sonido?
> ¿Por qué en tan bella y divinal mañana
> Lloro yo con dolor desconocido?
> ¡Es por tu muerte respetable anciana
> Que el eco hiere mi cansado oído!
> Y de tu vida de virtudes llena
> Tendré eterno recuerdo, eterna pena.[3]

> Why is my soul touched by the bell that tolls
> with such a funereal sound?
> Why on such a beautiful and divine morning
> does an unfamiliar grief cause me to weep?
> It is because of your death, venerable lady,
> that the echo strikes my weary ears!
> And of your life, filled with virtue, I
> will have eternal memories, eternal sorrow.

Palma was fifteen years old when he wrote this poem and was attending the Convictorio de San Carlos. In these Romantic verses the poet emphasizes funeral bells, death, grief, and weeping. Of more than passing interest is the fact that in some lines not included here Palma seems to have a firm belief in a Christian deity. In a period of life when many young people begin to lose their religious faith, Palma is consoled by the conviction that this lady has found her place in God's kingdom. Palma's faith in a Christian deity remained strong throughout his life in spite of the assaults of science and Positivism against religious belief.

Palma's second poem honors Marshal Gamarra, one of Peru's military heroes; it was published in 1848.[4] In the one strophe I have been able to obtain the poet praised Gamarra in highly laudatory and very conventional language.

Possibly the next of his poems which are still in print is entitled "A un cisne" [To a Swan] and was published in 1849. Raúl Porras Barrenechea quotes some lines from this poem:

> Bien haya el ave a quien la blanca espuma
> El puro nácar de los mares vende. . . .
> Que si tú lloras desdenes
> Ya congoja te mata
> También sufro de una ingrata
>   El desamor.
> Igual, cisne, es nuestro canto
> Y cuando cese mi llanto
> Une tu canto a mi canto
>   De dolor.[5]

> Hail the bird to whom the white foam lends
> The glistening beauty of the mother of pearl. . . .
> For if you weep over the disdain you suffer
> And anguish kills you
> I also suffer lack of love because of an
>   ungrateful woman.
> Our song, swan, is the same
> And when my lament ceases
> Join your song with my song
>   Of grief.

Three points should be made concerning these verses. First, the lines are of varying length. Such experimentation in versification is evidence of Palma's Romantic bent. In the first poem he wrote all of the lines are eleven syllables long and in the second there are fourteen syllables in each verse. In this period as he continued to write he innovated more in the versification. Second, this third poem is sprinkled with Romantic words such as *lloras* ("thou weepest), *congoja* ("anguish"), *sufro* ("I suffer"), *llanto* ("weeping"), and *dolor* ("sorrow"). In fact, especially in the second portion, the emphasis is Romantic, with stress placed on death, anguish, and unhappy love. Third, the subject of the poem is a swan, the same graceful bird which became a symbol of Modernism. It is apparent that many years before Rubén Darío wrote about swans they appeared in the poetry of a Peruvian Romantic poet.

Palma's heavy, serious style changes in his next poem, "Báquicas" [Bacchanalia]. In it he tells how Ovid, the poet of love, became very depressed on one occasion when he couldn't find his wine bag. Palma then tells how happy life becomes when there is something to drink and finishes the poem telling us that there is only one thing he envies—the cup which his lady love drinks from. For the first time in his poetry we find a light tone, especially when he makes fun of Ovid, whom he refers to as a *babieca* ("dolt"), a colloquial expression which is evidence of the fact that at this early age (Palma was about fifteen or sixteen years old) he did not feel that language always had to be elegant or proper.

Palma's interest in drama is brought out in "La comedia casera. Quevedo a Zorrilla" [A Homely Play. Quevedo to Zorrilla], which was published in 1850. In it he makes fun of students who put on plays upon the completion of final examinations. In Palma's opinion, the performances, mostly of plays written by José Zorrilla, were very bad indeed, and in his poem he depicts Quevedo, who is in Hell, weeping over the sad fate of Zorrilla, whose plays have been ruined by the inept students. This poem caused such a furor that Palma feared for his safety, to the extent that he was afraid to leave his home for fear of being tossed in a blanket. The impasse was not resolved until the rectors of the schools intervened. In this poem we enjoy the satirical tone, the portrayal of Hell, the grotesque images, and the picturesque, colloquial language. Here are some lines from the poem. Quevedo says to Zorrilla:

Con los diablicos me estaba
durmiendo muy sosegado
cuando escucho que estallaba
tal gresca que enojos daba
al diablo más endiablado.
Era que entre bastidores
pintados a mamarrachos,
con músicos rascadores,
con recios apuntadores,
farsa hacían los muchachos.
Juan Tenorio dan aquí;
acá *El rey y el zapatero;*
un papamoscas ví allí;
acá rey de turbio cuero;
y triste lloré por ti.[6]

I was sleeping very peacefully
with the little imps
when I heard such a rumpus
breaking out that it enraged
the most devilish devil.
The thing was that behind the scenes
painted in a ridiculous fashion
with musicians scraping on their instruments,
and loud prompters, the boys
were putting on a farce.
Here they present *Juan Tenorio*
and over here *The King and the Shoemaker;*
a simpleton saw I there;
and here a king in dark leather;
and sadly I cried for you.

Two years later Palma published a long poem which reveals that
his attention was being attracted to the past. "Flor de los cielos"
[Flower of the Heavens] was inspired by a poem written by a
Colombian in exile, Julio de Arboleda, who wrote a poem based on a
fictionalized version of the exploits of a conquistador who soldiered
with Francisco Pizarro in Peru and later fought alongside Gonzalo
Pizarro when the latter rebelled against the Crown. Palma knew
Arboleda very well and was very impressed with the Colombian's
poem entitled "Gonzalo de Oyón." Arboleda's poem had a historical

foundation; Palma's did not. He merely concocted a narrative about a Spaniard who fell in love with an Indian girl, named Flower of the Heavens. She returned his love but rejected his offer to marry her, saying that Indian tradition would not allow her participation in the marriage ceremony. After living with Flower for a period of time the Spaniard abandoned her. Later when he was about to leave on a military expedition Flower entreated him to return to her and their child. When he refused she stabbed him to death and then committed suicide by hurling herself from a cliff.

Palma expresses some of his opinions about some interesting topics in "Flower of the Heavens." He expresses love for his country, rails against the Spanish conquistador who came seeking gold, and laments the fact that the Incas bowed down before them. The poet applauds Flower's determination not to get married and states that two people who fall in love are married and have no need of a ceremony. Further, he maintains that when a man and a woman get married they soon get tired of each other and their home becomes a hell. This attitude seems to be one which was characteristic of Palma until relatively late in life, for he was forty-three years old when he married. Another point which deserves mention is that Palma digresses at a particular juncture and then defends what he has done. This is what he wrote: "Perdonadme si aquí vuelvo a mi añeja/Costumbre de meterme en digresiones;/Sin digresiones no es buena una conseja,/ Como no lo es un drama sin bribones. . ."[7] ("Pardon me if at this point I return to my old custom of digressing. Without digressions a tale is no good, just like a drama without scoundrels"). Countless "tradiciones" attest to the fact that this was no idle statement; his narratives contain a generous number of digressions. In fact, his desire to comment on the topic at hand and insert historical paragraphs helps to make the "tradición" a new genre, different from a short story. In the poem as a whole many Romantic elements may be noted. Among them are the emphasis on America, patriotism, a return to the colonial past, impossible love, powerful emotions, and an emphasis upon Nature. In Palma's early career Nature was emphasized in many of his works; in his mature years it plays an insignificant role in his prose as well as his poetry. Here are two strophes from "Flower of the Heavens" in which Nature is described in some detail.

La luna melancólica cruzaba
Por entre nubes el azul cielo,
Y su faz amarilla rïelaba
En el terso cristal del arroyuelo.

El aura mece las alzadas copas
Del verde sauce y del ciprés amigo;
Y van las aves en pintadas tropas
A buscar en sus ramas abrigo.[8]

The melancholy moon crossed the
Azure sky between the clouds,
And its yellow face glittered in
The glassy water of the stream.

A gentle breeze sways the lofty tree top
Of the green willow and its friend the cypress;
And the birds, in painted flocks, go off
To seek shelter in the branches.

A study of the language of the poem reveals many Romantic words. Some of the principal categories are (1) words of emotion; (2) words of the ideal; (3) words related to death; (4) references to American things, places, and personages; (5) words related to Nature; and (6) words related to fate. Indianisms are very rare in the poem. Peruvianisms do not seem to attract Palma very much during this stage of his career; just a few years later his attitude would change

This poem is related in an interesting way to one of Palma's "tradiciones," "El hermano de Atahualpa" [Atahualpa's Brother]. Written one year after "Flower of the Heavens" this "tradición" had its setting in the period of the conquest and dealt with the drama which developed when a Spanish conquistador lusted after a young Indian woman who was in love with a young Indian. The plot develops differently as we have already seen in Chapter 3, but there is emphasis on Nature, the ending is tragic, and there are many Romantic tones. One feature of the prose piece which distinguishes it from the poem is that there are several Indianisms. They reveal that at this point Palma is becoming interested in words that originated in the indigenous background of Peru, a lexicographic interest which would become more and more significant as the years went by. It is safe to say that this poem points in the direction which Palma will travel when he begins his search for literary fame. His "tradiciones" would become a powerful evocation of Peru's colonial past which would be an artistic creation composed of fiction and history.

The poem "Amargura" [Bitterness] shows us a philosophical side of the poet and sheds a bit of light on his childhood. One complete strophe and part of another follow:

> Yo sé que hay una farsa a que asistimos
> Todos los que a la vida despertamos,
> Y sin saberlo acaso recibimos
> Algún papel que en ella ejecutamos.
> En ella unos de gala nos vestimos,
> Otros la ropa del mendigo usamos. . .
> Sociedad denominan esa farsa
> De la que son los hombres la comparsa.
>
> También soy infeliz; que la fortuna
> Me hizo el acíbar apurar inmundo,
> Desde que al rayo de la blanca luna
> Sin sueños de oro y con dolor profundo
> Huérfano el corazón gimió en la cuna. . . .[9]

> I know there is a farce we all attend,
> All who wake up in the morning of this life.
> And without being aware of it
> We are assigned some role that we play.
> In it we dress sometimes in finery
> And sometimes in a beggar's rags. . .
> Society we call that farce of which men
> Are a troop of masqueraders.
>
> I also am unhappy; fate has forced me
> To drain the cup of repugnant aloes
> Since the time when, bathed in the beams
> Of a white moon, without golden dreams
> And with profound anguish, my orphan heart
>   whimpered in the cradle. . . .

The first strophe echoes the well-known "Life is a stage" concept which Shakespeare made famous; the second one hints that during

Palma's childhood he was bereft of his mother's attention. Because he took great pains to keep this part of his life a secret the accuracy of this allusion is difficult to judge. However, it is significant that Palma never referred to his mother.

Another interesting poem of this first period is "Fragmento de un diario" [Fragment of a Diary], because the last strophes focus on the young poet's first romantic entanglement. Although her name does not appear in the poem, the young woman Palma addresses in these lines is probably Teresa, the girl who caused a crisis in his life. As we have noted in Chapter 1, Palma had to choose between marrying her and going to sea. He chose the latter. He declares his overwhelming love to her and then says that the world cannot understand such passion because there is so much meanness and treason everywhere. What are they to do in a world in which passions are sold and illusion is omnipresent? He must continue on his gloomy road, a pilgrim who has lost his way, but he will bless her for the influence she has had on him.

Palma's growing disillusionment concerning his country is evident in "Enrique Alvarado," in which he laments the untimely passing of his friend. Alvarado, a gifted orator and writer, had been a bright hope for the future, and Palma holds him up as an example and excoriates the young people of Peru who are apathetic and worship the golden calf of personal gain. With the faith and enthusiasm demonstrated by Alvarado they must shatter the golden calf and fight for virtue. This theme is continued in "La juventud se divierte" [The Young People Amuse Themselves]. In Palma's opinion the youth of his country are interested only in having a good time; the problems Peru faces are overlooked or ignored. He harshly criticizes conditions in his country when he states that there is no government in Peru, just despotism, a fatal gangrene which the youth will not be able to cure. The younger generation is like dolls made of almond-flavored sugar paste who entertain themselves and get drunk at a carnival. But there are some young people who have faith in republican government and they will have their carnival some day at the expense of stupid charlatans who sow anarchy. "La troncha" [The Sinecure], the last poem to be treated in this division, appeared in 1859. Whereas Palma's criticism of the political situation had been quite indirect and never personal, it becomes both direct and personal in this poem.

President Castilla is depicted as a *tronchero* ("giver of sinecures") who
has given out so many "soft" jobs that Peru has compromised its
honor. As a result, Palma states in an ironic tone, his miserable nation
gets along very well. He denounces the guano industry, which Castilla
had developed, and, making use of an invented word, "enhuanas"
(approximate meaning—you cover with guano), addresses guano as if
it were a person, curses it, and says in essence the heart of his country
has been polluted with bird manure. Then he declares that in some
ways the colonial past is superior to the republican present. These are
his words:

> ¡El honor! Tal vez antaño
> no era el encontrarle extraño. . .
> El honor por Belcebú!
> no es fruta que en el Perú
> pueda aclimatarse ogaño.[10]

> Honor! Perhaps in the past
> it wasn't strange to find you. . .
> Honor, by Beelzebub!
> is not a fruit that can find a
> favorable climate nowadays in Peru.

The attitude expressed in these lines shows us that while still a young
man Palma was beginning to feel that the present was flawed and
corrupt and that the colonial past, in spite of stifling authoritarianism
and religious fanaticism, could boast of some virtues absent in the
Peru Ricardo Palma knew. This kind of attitude pointed him in the
direction of his "tradiciones" and would be expressed directly and
indirectly many times in the future. In 1860, one year after these last
two poems were published, Palma became involved in the abortive
attempt to assassinate President Castilla and was exiled to Chile. The
liberal views he expressed in his poetry were no pose; a true Romantic,
he wanted changes in literature and politics and was not afraid to
express himself openly and act in a forthright manner.

1860–1870

This division is composed of the following collections: *Juvenilia*
(1860), *Armonías* [Harmonies, 1865], and *Pasionarias* [Passionflow-

ers, 1870].[11] All of them are extremely Romantic in theme, style and form; very rarely do we detect a tone that is humorous or convivial. Typical themes are love, pain, disillusionment, and God.

In the first volume, *Juvenilia,* Palma is pessimistic, amorous, disillusioned, and inquisitive. There is little of the whimsical writer we see in the "tradiciones" but there is one poem in which he combines a serious tone with a light one—"Poema en cuatro sonetos" [A Poem in Four Sonnets]. The subjects of the four sonnets are philosophy, love, the fatherland, and suicide. The poet asks questions about the nature of the first three of these topics and receives the same basic answer for all of them—there is no answer. In the last sonnet Palma departs from the pattern established in the first three. No questions are posed by Palma; he merely comments on the emptiness of life. He complains that he hasn't had one serene hour of happiness; he has no friend or lover to console him and he never lacks for some fool who wants to tell him his troubles. The poet's fate is certain—he must end it all by taking his life. The next line exhibits an ironic twist when the poet states: "Pero antes tomaremos chocolate" ("But first, let's have a drink of chocolate").[12]

One poem in *Armonías* is a narrative piece which could have become a "tradición." In "Romance" we are told that during the period of the Inca Empire one of the Incas could go to sleep only if a linnet would sing for him. Unfortunately for the bird its song was too cheerful for the unhappy ruler, who wanted to hear only mournful warblings. The Inca, therefore, plucked out the bird's eyes; whereupon the linnet sang sad songs and finally died singing heavenly songs. There are many "tradiciones" which have a very weak plot or none at all. On the slight narrative frame presented in this poem Palma could possibly have created a "tradición" if he had been so inclined.

Another significant poem in this collection is "Navegando" [Sailing], which became popular in Spanish America because of the Romantic sentiments expressed by the poet while leaving Peru for exile. This is the very poem Rubén Darío, the High Priest of Modernism, loved so much. In an article on Palma found in Darío's *Obras completas* he stated that one of his childhood dreams had been to stand in the presence of the poet who had written *Armonías,* because from his early years he had enjoyed the poem "Sailing."[13] Exoticism is rare in Palma's poetry, but there is a good example of it in this volume. "Oriental" is a poem in which he talks of shawls of Kashmir, the purple of Tyre, perfume from Istanbul, and pearls from Golconda as he praises the beauty of a young lady he refers to as his Nazarene.

There is a lack of the lightness characteristic of his "tradiciones." It is true that toward the end of the collection there is a group of poems placed under the heading "Cantarcillos" [Little Ballads], in which Palma is less serious than in the other poems of the collection, but we are still far from the jovial playful Palma. In these verses the poet depicts a dialogue between a mother and a daughter in which the mother threatens to whip her young daughter because she likes to while away the hours after curfew talking with the barber. The daughter protests that her mother has forgotten her youthful days and that no woman can resist sweet words of love spoken by a young man. A few lines suffice to indicate the tone. The mother says:

> Con Lucas el barberillo
> hace dos noches o tres,
> que tú, al toque de la queda,
> das en salir, Isabel
> a platicar en la puerta
> y eso, chica, no está bien.
> Ve que si esto se repite, si esto
> vuelve a suceder;
> *te arrimo una buena felpa*
> o te corto el pelo. . . . (*Poesías
>   completas*, p.88)

> For two or three nights, Isabel,
> you have been talking
> in the doorway with
> Lucas, the young barber,
> after curfew, and, that,
> my dear girl, is not good.
> Now look, if this happens again
> I will whip you soundly, or
> I will cut off your hair.

The daughter replies:

Madre, en tus tiempos perdidos
que acaso ha olvidado usted
pudo resistirse a voces
de: —chica te quiero bien;
serás mi media naranja,
pimpollito de clavel,
y por ti me prevarico,
cual por el agua la sed—
dichas por algún mozo
con retintín y altivez! (*Poesías completas,* p. 89.)

Mother, in your youthful years
that perhaps you have forgotten,
could you resist words such as:
"My dear, I love you deeply;
you will be my better half,
my little carnation bud,
I need you desperately,
just as thirst needs water"—
words uttered by a fine young man
in a vibrant and proud tone!

We notice with interest that the expressions: "te arrimo una buena felpa" ("I will whip you soundly"), "serás mi media naranja" ("you will be my better half"), and "pimpollito de clavel" ("my little carnation bud") lend a familiar note to the poem and remind us of similar expressions scattered through the "tradiciones." Another portion of the poem "Cantarcillos" describes a woman in a manner that reminds the reader of Palma's famous prose pieces:

Oh niña, niña, niña,
   la del tontillo
hueco cual la cabeza
   de los Ministros.
¿Sabes esta mañana
   lo que me han dicho?
Que por ti en los infiernos
   hay infinitos;

pues son tan tentadores
   tus ojos lindos
que harán pecar a un santo
   del cielo mismo.
Cuando a la calle sales
   ¡qué cuerpo, Cristo!
¡y qué pie tan remono,
   tan repulido!
y luego un zarandeo
   tan subversivo!
Por eso contemplándote
   un fraile dijo:

Tus pecados mortales
   son tan bonitos
que yo, aunque me condene,
   te los bendigo. (*Poesías completas,*
p. 95)

Oh little girl, little girl, little girl
   you whose hoop skirt
is as hollow as the heads of
   our Cabinet Members.
Do you know what I was told
   this morning?
That because of you there are
   many souls in Hell.
Your lovely eyes are
   so tempting
that they would cause to sin
   a saint straight from Heaven.
   When you walk on the street,
   Lord, what a figure!
And what cute feet so
   tastefully arrayed!
And then such subversive
   strutting!
That's why a friar remarked
   upon looking you over:
Your mortal sins
   are so beautiful

> *that even though I'm condemned*
> *for it, I bless them.*

Palma's appreciation for the women of Lima is apparent in his poetry as well as his prose. The interesting thing about such descriptions is that the reader comes away from Palma's writings feeling that the women described are indeed lovely and attract just about every male who sees them, regardless of his rank, vocation, or marital status. A careful scrutiny of these descriptions reveals, however, that few details are provided and some that are given are conventional and are often repeated. The effectiveness of Palma's descriptions of *limeñas* probably should be attributed more to his clever use of words than to skillful, detailed descriptions of them.

Several poems in *Passionflowers* deserve our attention because they demonstrate the poet's interest in contemporary events. In "¡A las armas!" [To Arms!] he castigates France for its intervention in Mexico (1861–1867); in "Al mariscal Castilla" [To Marshal Castilla] he praises the accomplishments of the president who sent him into exile; and in "Armonía bíblica" [Biblical Harmony] he eulogizes his dear friend José Gálvez, who suffered a hero's death at Callao during the war with Spain in 1867. Three other poems merit comment because they are different from the majority of the others. "Romanticismo" is a poem in which the author makes fun of himself. He tries to impress a girl with very Romantic, trite language. She listens to him, and then tells him to try his line on someone else. Here are some verses from the poem:

> Eres ángel venido de otra esfera
> la tierra a engalanar con tu hermosura:
> de matinal estrella la luz pura
> en tu dulce mirada reverbera. (*Poesías completas,* p. 112)

> You are an angel who has come
> to adorn the earth with your beauty:
> the pure light of the morning star
> vibrates in your sweet glance.

After a few more flattering lines of this kind the sonnet closes with this tercet:

—Tal dije a Carmen. No mordió el anzuelo,
y contestó: —¡palabras de poeta!
Vaya usted con la música a otra parte.
                    (*Poesías completas*, p. 113)

That's what I said to Carmen. She didn't bite,
instead she answered, "Words of a poet.
Try your line on someone else."

The tone is a mocking one and it is interesting that Palma presents himself as an unsuccessful suitor whose Romantic entreaties are ignored.

Perhaps the poem which tells us most about Palma the writer is "A Florencio Escardó" [To Florencio Escardó] because for the first time he expresses his preference for the past over the present in a categoric manner. Palma takes his good friend Escardó to task for castigating the past and, in addition, scoffs at Escardó's opinion that human beings have improved and are much superior to their grandfathers. Men don't change, says Palma. They still fight, there are still social problems, and one science overshadows all the rest—the exploitation of human beings by other human beings. The first strophe is a self-portrait of Palma in which we see him poring over his dusty chronicles when Escardó's letter arrives:

Haciendo guerra a la infernal polilla
y asfixiándome el polvo los pulmones,
arrellanado estábame en la silla
descifrando unos rancios cronicones,
cuando entró mi criado, y en silencio,
entregóme tu carta, buen Florencio.
                    (*Poesías completas*, p. 137)

While I was fighting with some accursed moths
and asphyxiating myself with dust
from some musty old chronicles
I was reading while curled up in my chair,
in came a servant
and silently handed me your letter.

The exact date of this composition is not available, but it is evident that by 1870, two years before he published the First Series of *Tradiciones*, Palma had begun to bury his life in the past and was defending his love for the past against those who preferred the present.

Although the versification in this volume continues to reveal Palma's Romantic tendency to experiment, the poet uses more and more of the traditional forms. The verse form used most often is the *romance*; not far behind are the *serventesio* and the *redondilla*. It is safe to say that Romanticism in Palma's verses is beginning to wane in some ways and in other ways it is becoming stronger. In his desire to immerse himself in the past in his investigations and in his writing he found himself moving in a very Romantic direction which would eventually lead him to his portrayal of the colonial past in his *Tradiciones*. At the same time in style, theme and versification he moves away from Romanticism, although we don't see any abrupt change until we read Palma's next collection.

1870–1892

Three volumes of poetry are included in this division. They are *Verbos y gerundios* [Verbs and Present Participles, 1877], *Nieblas* [Mists, 1886], and *Filigranas* [Filigrees, 1892].[14] This is the period during which Palma launched his prose writing career in earnest and established himself as a significant literary figure. The poems in *Verbs and Present Participles* were written between 1870 and 1877, during which Palma published the first four series of *Tradiciones*. During these years he rejects the Romantic narrative and the very short novel and develops the witty, satirical, and lively style characteristic of his literary maturity. We note with interest that the poems of this period also underwent significant changes. In a preface to the volume Carlos Augusto Salaverry, a Peruvian writer, stated the following: "If you like to see disheveled hair, faces that are always pale, eyes that are always somber and wet from lachrymose poetry, we do not advise that you read *Verbos y gerundios*. This is a collection of light verse, festive, epigrammatic, and above all, sparkling. It is a book written in moments of good humor to be read in hours of amusement."[15]

The first poem, "La última copita" [The Last Small Drink], is characteristic of the tone of this volume. The poet tells about meeting a man who is intoxicated because he had been drinking brandy in a neighboring bar. However, in spite of the fact that he had consumed twenty cups, he was still clear headed. But as he was about to leave, the owner treated him to one last drink, and that, not the first twenty cups, had made him drunk. Life is like that, says Palma, in a strophe of commentary. We have a series of difficulties beset us and then along comes one crowning blow, which we then blame for all our woes. As human beings we tend to forget the first twenty drinks and blame intoxication on the last small drink; in a like manner when something terrible happens to us we blame the last incident and forget about the many events and unsolved problems which led up to the disaster. Another poem, "Heroicidad" [Heroism], also treats the theme of alcohol. An inveterate drinker had sworn he would drink no more, whereupon a friend who could not believe that his drinking buddy was sincere took him to a bar and ordered drinks for the two of them. The reformed drinker continued to reject any suggestion that he take a drink and felt very proud of himself. His pride continued to grow until he compared himself to Napoleon. The climax was reached when he told himself that the heroic act of overcoming such a powerful temptation deserved a fitting reward—a drink of brandy! In a satirical tone Palma notes one of our human weaknesses. "Pride goeth before the fall," states one of our well-known proverbs. In Palma's poem there is a neat twist. Not only does the reformed drinker fall, he falls by doing the very thing that his "heroic" abstention had brought into being—pride in becoming a teetotaler. Thus we have a vicious cycle in which the drinker develops a serious blind spot. The poem presents the situation in such a way that the reader chuckles and pities the "reformed" individual who by false reasoning returns to his old ways. But how many of us are guilty of the same type of behavior without realizing how ridiculous and illogical we really are? Who will tell us how silly we sometimes are? Where is the poet or some other observer who is able to paint us as others see us?

The new Palma still writes about love, but not in the cloying, sentimental, emotional way characteristic of his earlier verses. "A una beata" [To a Very Zealous Churchwoman] is the story of Santa Nefita, who lived in the reign of Diocletian, one of the Roman emperors (A.D. 245–313). She was sentenced to be exiled because she refused to give up her religion. While traveling to her destination she reached a river and because she carried no money with her she paid for the passage with a kiss, given to the ferryman. Later on, she gave kisses for bread and alms. She was truly a charitable woman. The poet tells this story to a young girl, who asked, "Is that really true?" "Of course," replied the poet. "And if you want to be a saint, be charitable to me the way Santa Nefita was."[16] Another light poem of this type is "Galantería mística" [Mystical Gallantry], which tells of a patient in the hospital who, watching a pretty nurse attend to his needs, exclaims, "Good Lord!" Whereupon she said, "Don't take it so hard. I am His daughter. What can I do for you?" His reply was, "What do I want? That He accept me as his son-in-law" (*Poesías completas,* p. 188).

Firmly dedicated to the cause of bachelorhood as we have already seen, Palma finally succumbed to the charms of Cristina Román when he was forty-three years old. His public admission of surrender to the state of matrimony and his desertion from the ranks of the bachelors are contained in "Mi parte de matrimonio" [My Wedding Invitation], a poem which he included with his wedding announcements. In it he tells of his history of determined resistance to any thought of marriage and of his satisfaction with bachelorhood. Then he proclaims that the marriage bug has bitten him and that he is deserting bachelor ranks to become a husband. Two strophes are sufficient to give an idea of the nature of the poem.

> ¡Maridos! de mis ultrajes
> pasados no hagáis ya caso:
> a vuestro campo me paso
> con armas y con bagajes.
>
> Es cosa tradicional
> que, en este mundo embrollón,
> se empieza de oposición,
> se acaba ministerial. (*Poesías completas,* p. 227)
>
> Husbands! Pay no attention
> to my past outrages:
> I'm coming over to your side
> with weapons and equipment.

> It is a normal thing that
> in this messed-up world
> one begins with the opposition
> and ends up a member of the Cabinet.

Some of the other themes in this delightful collection are politics, liberty, vanity, death, and poetry itself. One poem in the volume, "Intimidades" [Intimacies], is a very significant one, for in it he once again expresses his preference for the past, and, in addition, states that Juan Martínez Villergas, whom he had met in England some twelve years before, had influenced his writing in a marked way. After referring to the political struggles and disillusionments in which both of them had played their roles, Palma traces his literary successes, placing emphasis on the dusty documents he had perused and on the *Anales* [Annals] and the *Tradiciones* he had published. He then wrote the following:

> Yo me apliqué al pasado. Tú al presente,
> mi maestro y amigo, Y no te asombre
> saber que debo a ti, principalmente,
> la muy modesta fama de mi nombre.
> Que tú el primero en revelarme fuiste,
> en plática amistosa, cuan galana
> es y cual pompa y majestad reviste
> la deliciosa lengua castellana. (*Poesías completas*, p. 230)

> I applied myself to the past. You to the present,
> teacher and friend. And don't be surprised
> to learn that to you more than any other,
> I owe my very modest fame.
> For you were the first one to reveal to me
> in friendly conversation how elegant
> is the magnificent Castilian language and
> with what pomp and majesty it is clothed.

Palma may have been guilty of flattery, but it may also be that the influence of Villergas was important and merits further attention.

The versification used in *Verbs and Present Participles* is revealing. There are fifty-three poems in the work and the *silva* is used twenty-seven times. The other traditional forms, none of which is employed more than three times, are the *serventesio*, the *quintilla*, the *redondilla*, the *cuarteto*, and the sonnet. Although there is one example of free verse, in general we must say that Palma is no longer the experimenter, the breaker of rules, the Romantic rebel in his versification. In his first three collections he used traditional verse forms approximately 30 percent of the time. In this last volume he used them about 75 percent of the time.

Nieblas [Mists]

According to Palma this volume of poetry, his last important one, was written during a period when he wrote poetry only when others insisted that he write something for them or when poetry alone could express certain ideas with the elegance they deserved. These poems were written between 1880 and 1886, a period during which Palma wrote about 330 "tradiciones." Although the whimsical tone has not disappeared completely, the poet is more serious, more thoughtful, and more cognizant of the somber mists of the spirit. He is pessimistic in "En la última página del *Quijote*" [On the Last Page of the *Quijote*] and in "Prosa rimada" [Rhymed Prose]. In the first the poet states that mankind is still as mad as Don Quixote was and in the second he maintains that where there are tyrants the people who cower under their rule deserve them because of their cowardice and their decadence. And what is more, ruling despots are all right where they are, for the Genghis Khans and the Attilas have their roles to play. He is satirical in "Lavandería" [The Laundry], in which he refers to the confessional as a patented laundry of souls. Souls are like shirts and must be spotlessly clean in Heaven, where cleanliness is one of the great virtues. His tone is eulogistic in "Condolencias patrióticas" [Patriotic Condolences], in which he praises three Peruvians killed in the War of the Pacific, two of whom were the great heroes Miguel Grau and Alfonso Ugarte. The former, an admiral, died in a naval engagement fighting a superior Chilean naval force; the latter, rather than surrender the flag he loved so much, wrapped himself in it, and riding his fiery horse to the edge of a cliff, cast himself and his horse into the sea. Books are praised and libraries are called temples in "En la Biblioteca" [In the Library]. One of his longest poems, "A San Martín," has two purposes—to pay homage to the great Argentine general and to denounce wars carried on between Spanish American nations. Although no mention is made of Chile, that country felt that it was the target of some of Palma's accusations and a protest was lodged by the Chilean government with the government of Peru.

Poems of a lighter tone are "Album" and 'Análisis." In the first, the poet says that he would be rich if he were to steal the jewels attributed to a certain young lady in decadent verses found in her album. He could rob her of her rubies (lips), and her pearls (teeth), and by selling them to a jeweler could escape from his state of poverty. The second poem, a variation on a theme by Bartrina, castigates the analytical approach to learning. The poet analyzed the style of a certain journalist and found copper instead of gold. Even theology cannot withstand analysis. From analysis rises doubt, which in turn gives way to negation, which leads to Hell. Nothing can resist analysis, for even in the sun and in the most beautiful girl defects can be found. Therefore, we should forget about analysis. The motto for progress is "Synthesis," not "Analysis." Here is the last strophe. (Ricardo is a friend of his.)

> Por eso es lo mejor no requemarse
> con averiguaciones,
> y pasar sobre mil y mil cuestiones
> como sobre ascuas para no quemarse.
> Lo demás es romperse las narices
> para luego salir por la tangente.
> Si quieres ser dichoso, francamente,
> no analices, Ricardo, no analices. (*Poesías completas*, p. 241)

> And so it is best not to get all excited
> about digging out answers but to pass lightly
> over myriads of problems as if you were walking
> on redhot coals, so you won't get burned.
> To do anything beyond that is to beat your head
> against a wall, Ricardo, and fly off at a tangent.
> If you want to be happy, frankly,
> don't analyze, Ricardo, don't analyze.

Another noteworthy poem in this collection is "Lectura" [Reading], written for the inauguration of the Ateneo de Lima. The theme of these verses is *"la limeña,"* the woman of Lima. He describes her in great detail, comments on her personality, and, in short, explains why she is such a captivating creature. There is a rare phosphoresence in her eyes, her figure is slim and willowy, and her bosom is firm and prominent. When she smiles, she caresses; when she laughs, she enchants; when she speaks, her words turn into poetry. Many and varied are her moods. She can be a stout rock that withstands all assaults; her glory, like that of cherubs; her anger, like a hurricane; and her disdain, like the Andean snow. Her love hides volcanic fire; she dazzles, attracts, sears, and casts spells. She is generous, altruistic, charitable, always smiling and amiable. And whether she is at a party or keeping vigil at someone's deathbed, she is always affable. Such was the praise Palma showered upon this fascinating person. It is small wonder that he wrote so much about her and in such glowing terms.

A study of the versification reveals that the *silva* is once again the most popular form. Others noted are *décimas, redondillas,* sonnets, *serventesios, cuartetas, octavas reales,* and *romances,* including some slight variations of the latter form. Of the thirty-five poems, nineteen are cast in traditional forms (forms which show no variation from the types of versification outlined in treatises of Spanish versification in which orthodox forms are presented).

Filigranas [Filigrees, 1886–1892]

This last collection consists of poems he wrote for albums and other social obligations. They add little to Palma's reputation as a poet. Only two hundred copies were printed and these were sent to friends as a type of *aguinaldo* (New Year's gift). The tone of this poetry runs the gamut from playfulness to serious advice and thoughtful comments on life. Of course, the lighter tone is much more in evidence than the serious one. In this volume there are many very short poems, of which the following are representative examples:

> En toda enfermedad hay un microbio:
> en la de amor, el novio. (*Poesías completas,* p. 311)

> In every illness there is a microbe:
> in the illness of love that microbe is the lover.

> Todo hombre de talento
> tiene su cuarto de hora de jumento. (p. 293)

Every talented man
has his quarter of an hour as an ass.

Se le fue la mano al cura parroquial,
pues te puso, al bautizarte, mucha sal. (p. 307)

The priest got carried away when he baptized you
because he placed a lot of salt on your head.

The popularity of Palma's "tradiciones" was and is so great that his poetry has been largely ignored. But the value to be derived from its study is not insignificant. For example, we can see that his poetry reflects faithfully the two poles of his poetic nature. At first, he was a typical Romantic who wrote lyrical effusions about love and disillusionment and related themes. He was not original in his ideas or in his style, although he did experiment considerably with verse forms. A seemingly sudden change took place during the years 1870–1877, the period during which he wrote the poems published in *Verbs and Present Participles*. He is still disillusioned and he still writes about love, but he has rejected Romanticism. In this volume he is irreverent, whimsical, satirical, and festive. He is less formal in this poetry (in some cases he is actually chatty), he uses colloquial and slang expressions, and in general he makes an attempt to portray the spoken language of the people. And beginning with this volume, as has been noted, he prefers to use the more conventional verse forms.

In conclusion, Palma's poetry provides us another point of view from which to observe his literary career. It is possible to see in his "tradiciones" some Romanticism, but it is impossible to see the transition from Romanticism to a more realistic kind of expression. In our study of his prose we noted that Palma very diligently sought to eliminate Romanticism by doing three things, rewriting Romantic pieces, eliminating ones that could not be revised, and changing the chronological order in the definitive edition of his *Tradiciones*. Evidently when Palma prepared his definitive edition of his poetry he was not concerned about what critics might say about his verses. His reputation had been firmly established on his prose; his poetry, which he himself belittled, would serve to illuminate his period of initiation in the world of letters. The Romanticism which he had sought to conceal in his "tradiciones" is spotlighted in his poetry. In his verses we see his early Romanticism, the lessening of it and also the almost complete lack of it in his last collections. His other works furnish us with valuable information about Palma and his literary pursuits, but there are facets of his personality that are found only in his poetry and others even highlighted in his poems.

Ricardo Palma—Linguist

From the very beginning of his writing career Palma demonstrated a love for and a great interest in the Spanish language. On one occasion he stated that the only good thing that the Spaniards brought to the New World was their language. He boasted of the fact that he had been made a corresponding member of the Royal Spanish Academy, and, further, he stated that in his complete edition of the *Tradiciones*, some 1,000 pages, he had been guilty of writing only about a dozen incorrect sentences. Perhaps this is an exaggeration, but the claim proves that Palma was very sensitive to matters of correctness in language. His very early interest in lexicography is evident in "El hermano de Atahualpa" [Atahualpa's Brother], his second extant work, published in 1852 and later entitled "La muerte en un beso" [Death in a Kiss]. In this juvenile work about tragic love in the time of the Conquest, Palma uses expressions such as *quena* (Quechua flutelike musical instrument made of reed), *ombú* (tree found only on the pampas of the Rio Plate region), and *tomeguín* (small bird native to Cuba). The tendency to use Americanisms was perhaps more Romantic than lexical in the early years of his career but later he rejected Romanticism as a literary tendency while placing more and more emphasis on lexicography. Two other early examples of the attraction of language for Palma are *Anales de la Inquisición* [Annals of the Inquisition] and "Palla Huarcuna," both published in 1860. In the *Annals* he pauses in his historical investigations in order to express his theory about the origin of the word "sambenito," the term used for the penitential garment worn by those punished by the Inquisition. According to Palma, the term originated in the fact that in the early years of the Holy Office most of the Inquisitors were monks of the Order of Saint Benedict and the victims of the Inquisition appeared before their judges in the monasteries of that order. "Palla-Huarcuna" is set in pre-Conquest times and tells of the death of a young slave girl who is put to death because she prefers to die with her lover rather than spend the rest of her life in the seraglio of the Inca Tupac-Yupanqui. Quechua terms used in this story are *llautu* (imperial tassel worn by the Inca or high dignitaries), *haravicus* (troubadors), *curacas* (potentates), and *guairuros* (trees whose fruit is used for making necklaces).

Perhaps the first work in which Palma's interest in language goes beyond a mere Romantic attraction for Americanisms is "Una carta de Indias" [A Letter from the Indies], first published in 1879. By this time he had written some 151 narrative prose pieces and had published four volumes of *Tradiciones*. The focus of this "tradición" is the avarice of one of the viceroys, Vaca de Castro, as it is revealed in a letter to his wife which was written in 1542. In a digression which is not related in any way to the viceroy, Palma discusses the origin of the word "America." He rejects the theory that it was derived from the name of the Italian navigator Amerigo Vespucci, stating that Vespucci's given name was really Albericus and that the New World should have been named Albericia if it had been named after Vespucci. He further points out that only royalty were privileged to have lands named after their given names; for example, Louisiana, Carolina, and Georgia received the first names of royalty but the Straits of Magellan, Vancouver Island, and Cook's Island were given the family names of their discoverers. It was Palma's contention that the name America is exclusively of New World origin and that it was the name of a place in Nicaragua, designating a range of mountains in the province of Chontales. The name was either America or Americ, according to Palma. The ending *ic* (*ica, ique, ico* in its Hispanized form), which is frequently found in Central America and the Antilles to designate places, means great, high, or prominent and is applied to mountains lacking volcanos. Palma's theory is that even though Columbus did not write the name in his letters, it was used by him and his companions and its use gradually became generalized in Europe. The name was of particular importance because gold was found in the America region of Nicaragua. Palma further theorizes that because the name was known in Europe in spite of the fact that documentation of its origin was unavailable, the name of ALBERICUS VESPUCCI was seized upon by Waldseemuller in 1508 as the origin of the place name "America" (Aguilar, p. 67).

A careful scrutiny of the rest of his "tradiciones" reveals a continuing interest in language and lexicography, but his zeal in this field reaches new heights toward the end of the century. In 1889 he wrote a letter to Daniel Granada, a friend living at the time in Montevideo, in which he expressed his gratitude for receiving a book entitled *Vocabulario platense* authored by Granada. Palma noted that many of the Argentinisms included therein were used with the same meanings in Peru and provided a list of ninety-six of these words. He also wrote that many of the words appeared in the latest edition of the dictionary of the Royal Spanish Academy because he had sent more than four hundred to that body and some three hundred had already been accepted.

Palma's attitude towards the academy became one of frustration when during his visit to Spain in 1892 he encountered an intransigent spirit with respect to the inclusion of additional Americanisms in the dictionary. Sharply critical of the conservatism of the members of the academy, he published a work in 1895, *Neologismos y americanismos*, in which he explained his antipathy toward that body. In this work he recognizes the important role the Spanish language has played in Spanish America and proudly notes that Spanish Americans have insisted on correct Spanish as much as the Spaniards themselves. To drive his point home he refers to the fact that some of the most brilliant scholars of the Spanish language were Spanish Americans and cites Andrés Bello, Rufino José Cuervo, and Rafael María Baralt. He then takes the academy to task for assuming a posture of superiority with respect to the Spanish spoken in Spanish America, complaining that it had refused to accept numerous words in widespread use in the New World and that it had insisted on its own spelling of certain Spanish American words. An example he provides is "México," spelled with an *x* in that country but a *j* in Spain. One of the points he makes with great feeling is that Spain and Spanish America could be brought closer together if the linguistic ties were strengthened. Unfortunately he believed that the opposite was taking place and that because of the animosity borne of the linguistic conflict the mother country and her offspring were drifting farther apart.

In the following section of the work he relates his experiences while in Spain and his disillusionment upon becoming aware that his proposals for the inclusion of some Americanisms in the dictionary merited such a negative reception. He had intended, he states, to present a few more than three hundred words to the academy but was so deeply disappointed after that body had rejected the first twelve that he refrained from proposing any more. There were some members who were sympathetic to Palma's suggestions, including Emilio Castelar, Ramón de Campoamor, Juan Valera, and Gaspar Núñez de Arce, but in spite of their support Palma felt that the rejections by the academy as a whole were systematic.

The final section of the work is a listing, together with definitions and linguistic discussions, of 509 neologisms and Americanisms he felt should be included in the academy dictionary. From our vantage point in 1980, it is revealing to determine how many of these words have now been clothed in the gown of respectability and accepted into the academy dictionary. According to the eighteenth edition of that work 343 words have now received the approval of the academy. Of the 166 not included, 102 are found in the *Pequeño Larousse*. Thus, 88 percent of the 509 words have been accepted by the academy and the *Larousse*; 68 percent have been accepted by the academy. Following are examples of words in the various categories according to their acceptance and rejection. The academy has accepted *agigantar, agredir, andino, aplomo, burocracia, cablegrama, casticidad, clausurar, cocaína, coloniaje, derrumbe, diagnosticar, editar, egotismo, enfocar, estampilla, oportunista, realización,* and *rifle.* Words found in the *Larousse* but not in the academy dictionary include *americanizar, carátula* (title page of book), *criollismo, curcuncho* (humpbacked), *defeccionarse, depreciar* (to depreciate in value), *imbebible, incásico,* and *motinista.* Some of the words still out are *aprovisionamiento, autodidaxia* (the ability to teach oneself), *cablegrafista, cabulista* (tricky, superstitious), *criollada,* and *jesuitismo.* The great majority of the Indian words he proposed were eventually accepted; most of the words rejected by the academy dealt with business, government, and literature. One interesting example of a word in this last category is "literatear," which means to attempt to make a career of writing without having the competence necessary for being successful.

Every speaker and writer of the Spanish language should be extremely grateful to Palma for his efforts to enrich the language. Words which we use every day, words which we now consider indispensable, received recognition and became respectable largely through the efforts of the "tradicionista." Not satisfied with the publication of *Neologismos y americanismos*, however, he published in 1903 another lexicographical work; this one was entitled *Papeletas lexicográficas (Dos mil setecientas voces que hacen falta en el Diccionario)* [Lexicographic Problems (Twenty-seven hundred Words the Dictionary Lacks)].

Rarely, especially in Spanish America, do we find a successful writer of fiction so deeply involved in the study of language who made contributions of note in that field. But this great interest should not surprise us because it explains, in part, his greatness. As has been stated before, style is responsible for Palma's amazing success and the developing of his style is due to his study and knowledge of the living language, of which he was a careful and zealous practitioner.

Because Palma the linguist was so important, this chapter would be incomplete without some of his fundamental ideas about language and some specific examples of how these ideas were translated into action. In "Gazapos oficiales" [Official Blunders] Palma wrote the following:

I never criticize the use of neologisms because I have always considered the Dictionary to be a measuring stick that is much too short. If in order to express my ideas I need to create a word, I don't bother about technicalities and I don't fret about scruples: I print it and that's that. For me, the spirit, the soul of the language lies in its syntax and not in the vocabulary. I even consider it a meritorious act, one worthy of high praise, to contribute new words to the enrichment of the language if those words are not formed arbitrarily. (Aguilar, pp. 1509–10)

To Juan María Gutiérrez he wrote the following:

What I don't want to see, my friend, is anarchy in the language. We were born speaking Spanish and we write in Spanish, but I don't want each country to have its own special dialect. The confusion of the tower of Babel would be fatal; what we should aspire to is the enriching of Spanish with the Americanisms in most general use.

Use and custom impose the adoption of words. . . .

My literary belief in its definitive form is that we can be *americanos* in the morality of ideas or the essence of what is written, but I don't conceive of the correctness of form as being in conflict with the language of Cervantes.[17]

Thus Palma fought for a correct Spanish but felt that the use of Americanisms and neologisms was legitimate. His measuring stick was the widespread use of a word; dogmatic or authoritarian attitudes were anathema to him.

Two examples demonstrate how severe he could be with those who were guilty of what he considered to be the use of incorrect language. In the first, the proofreader of some unnamed publishing house or periodical incurred his wrath for publishing the expression "bajo la base" instead of "bajo este pie" or "bajo esta base." After explaining his reasons for condemning the expression he wrote: "Daily I read in the official newspaper that concessions are made 'bajo las bases' and not 'sobre las bases.' It is true that there are no more recalcitrant enemies of correct language than important officials and section heads in the various ministries. If it is not possible to proscribe 'bajo las bases,' it will be necessary to allow it to subsist, thus adding it to the long list of idiocies authorized by the Academy. For such a petty thing the sky will not fall down on us."[18]

On another occasion he chastised the secretary of education, Wenceslao Valera, for using the term "consultador" instead of the accepted word "consultor." Palma pointed out that "consultador" was not in the fourteenth edition of the academy dictionary, while "consultor" had been in the dictionary since the fifteenth century. In his typical style he censured the secretary by writing the following: "I am fulfilling my Christian duty of informing you [of this] in order that neither the rubric of the President of the Republic nor the signature of his Secretary of Education will continue to authorize the use of such an absurd word."[19]

Although the linguistic facet of his career is little known and even less appreciated, it must be recognized and properly evaluated, for Palma's love affair with language was one of the most significant ingredients in the development of the "tradiciones."

Chapter Six
The Significance of
Ricardo Palma

Although many Spanish American writers felt the influence of Ricardo Palma and even wrote "tradiciones," none has surpassed him. In the words of the illustrious Chilean compiler of bibliographies José Toribio Medina: "Generally speaking, the man who is considered, and rightly so, the founder of this literary genre is Ricardo Palma, who published his first 'tradiciones' in Lima about 1873; Palma has remained the master whom all others have sought to follow, although it is only right to say it, at no time has anyone surpassed him, for there has not been anyone who has displayed such brilliant diction, such elegance in the telling of a story, and such variety in the scenes he was able to portray. . . ."[1]

The many writers who attempted to follow in his footsteps will now be noted and treated by country.

Mexico

General Vicente Riva Palacio wrote "tradiciones" treating the Conquest in which Cortés and his Indian lover, Doña Marina, appear in novelesque episodes. The titles of these works are *Tradiciones y leyendas en verso, El libro rojo* [The Red Book], and *México a través de los siglos* [Mexico through the Years]. Palma and Riva Palacio were very good friends, writing each other regularly from 1884 to 1892. On many occasions the Peruvian commented upon the general's works, showing special preference for those works which were similar to his own "tradiciones." In 1886 he wrote the following: "Your 'tradición' 'Consultar con la almohada' [Pillow Talk] is marvelously executed. But, do you know something, my friend? That 'tradición' is also Peruvian. We have it also; the protagonist is a bishop of Cuzco. I scribbled it, among others I did not consider worthy of my book, with the title 'Lo que pesa el oro en Oropesa' [What Gold Weighs in Oropesa]. Cultivate the vineyard of the 'tradición': you have no reason to expect anything but success and good harvest. You have literary talent to spare."[2] In the same year Palma wrote in another letter: "Your book *Tradiciones y leyendas en verso* has afforded me some very pleasant moments. You are one of the few poets I know about in our continent who are essentially American."[3]

More closely related to Palma's "tradiciones" are the narratives published by Luis González Obregón in *México viejo* [Old Mexico], circulated in series from 1891–1895. In 1892 Palma wrote to his friend informing him that he had read some of these articles with pleasure and commented on the fact that Mexico and Peru had a great deal in common with respect to the colonial past. What a rich vein of traditions remained unexploited, observed Palma. Later the same Mexican writer published *México anécdota* [Mexico: Anecdotes] and *Vetusteces* [Antiquities]. One of the "tradiciones" from the latter work was dedicated to Palma, who praised it and all other "tradiciones" González Obregón wrote. Another Mexican who penned works which were imbued with the spirit of the "tradiciones" was the Romantic poet Juan de Dios Peza. In his legends in verse he retold dramatic episodes which had occurred in the streets of Mexico City in the remote past. His purpose was to make known the reasons for which some of the city streets had been given such picturesque names.

Heriberto Frías, the novelist who wrote *Tomochic,* considered by many to be a significant precursor of the novels of the Mexican Revolution, was another writer of "tradiciones." His book *Leyendas históricas* (1899) contains narratives about life among the Indians in Mexico before the arrival of Cortés. Yet another Mexican who wrote "tradiciones" was Pedro Castera, who wrote pieces about mining days in Guanajuato and other mining centers.

Guatemala

Inspired by Palma's "tradiciones," Manuel Diéguez wrote four or five of his own which were well received in Guatemala and motivated the poet Juan Fermín Aycinena to write some pieces which had the spirit of the "tradición." Truly outstanding is the collection published by Agustín Mencos entitled *Crónicas de la antigua Guatemala* (1894). He emulated Palma by studying old documents of his country and then writing the more interesting episodes in a simple, correct style. Another writer of "tradiciones" was Antonio Batres Jaureguí, who published his *Memorias de antaño* [Memories of Long Ago] in New York in 1896. Batres Jaureguí, diplomat and friend of Palma, wrote very well according to Clemente Palma and Toribio Medina, and his "tradiciones" deserve recognition, but they lack the lightness characteristic of the "tradición" as Palma conceived it.[4]

Argentina

The most devoted and enthusiastic of Palma's disciples in Argentina was Pastor Obligado, who published four volumes of *Tradiciones argentinas*. He brought to light abundant material dealing with Argentina, but according to Clemente Palma, his style was lacking in care.[5] Only rarely, notes Medina, do we glimpse the magic of Palma's "tradiciones."[6] The only other Argentine worthy of mention here is Bernardo Frías, who published two volumes of *Tradiciones históricas de Salta*. Apparently they treated religious themes exclusively.

Chile

The first of the Chilean writers of "tradiciones" was Miguel Luis Amunátegui. Just two years after Palma published his First Series of "tradiciones" in 1872, Amunátegui began to publish some of his narratives in the newspaper *El Ferrocarril* [The Railroad]. Later they were collected and published under the title *Narraciones históricas*. The settings for his "tradiciones" were Peru, Mexico, and Chile. In his narratives he treated historical incidents about which there were still questions with respect to what really happened. Of the "tradiciones" set in Chile, Medina notes that some were rather dramatic and some had an erotic tone.[7] The next "traditionist" was Enrique del Solar, who published his *Leyendas y tradiciones* in two parts, the first in 1875 and the second in 1891. His pieces were based on incidents taken from Chilean history and Chilean tradition; however, some of the incidents he portrayed took place in distant countries, such as Spain. One "tradición" is especially interesting because in it he treats the duel that Alonso de Ercilla y Zúñiga, author of *La Araucana*, fought with Juan de Pineda. Not content with the historical outlines of the conflict, Solar makes use of his imagination to incorporate a love theme into the "tradición." Others who wrote similar narratives were Vicente Pérez Rosales *(Recuerdos del pasado* [Recollections of the Past]), Manuel Concha *(Tradiciones serenenses,)* Vicuña Mackenna, Justo Abel Rosales, Salvador Soto Rojas *(Crónicas chilenas)*, Joaquín Díaz Garces, Daniel Riquelme, and Aurelio Díaz Meza.

The last-named writer deserves marked attention because he published fifteen volumes of "tradiciones" under the general title *Leyendas y episodios chilenos.* He devoted five volumes to the Conquest, five to the colonial period, and five to the struggle for independence, a total of more than two hundred "tradiciones." Clemente Palma referred to him as a spiritual son of the great Peruvian "traditionist,"[8] for Díaz Meza had announced publicly that he intended to bring to fruition in Chile the same type of literary work Ricardo Palma had produced for Peru. In his introduction to the first volume of the series Díaz Meza wrote: "All these pieces constitute an inexhaustible treasure for the writer who is enamored by an attractive and mysterious past and who wishes to serve his country popularizing its social history whose details, which appear to be insignificant, give, generally speaking, an explanation of the greatest events."[9]

Peru

Ricardo Palma's own country has produced few writers of "tradiciones." Among those who deserve mention are José Antonio de Lavalle, who wrote some historical monographs, the poet José Gálvez, who wrote *Una Lima que se va* [A Lima That Is Fading Away], Aníbal Gálvez, author of some treatises dealing with Peruvian traditions, and Ismael Portal, a writer who depicted social and political life of a remote period.

Palma's most outstanding disciple was a woman, Clorinda Matto de Turner. Born near Cuzco in 1854, she married an Englishman, John Turner, in 1871. Attempting to imitate Palma, she submitted pieces to various newspapers. By 1875 the *Peru Courier* was publishing some of her "tradiciones" about Cuzco. In addition, Argentine magazines were printing some of these same pieces. Her husband died in 1881, and from that time on she devoted her efforts to literature and education. After becoming the editor of a newspaper in Arequipa she published her *Tradiciones cuzqueñas: Leyendas, biografías y hojas sueltas* [Traditions of Cuzco: Legends, Biographies and Loose Pages] during the years 1884-1886. Palma gave her considerable help and praised her highly. However, Luis Alberto Sánchez states that her pieces lacked the roguishness so characteristic of Palma's "tradiciones." The tone more typical of her narratives was a dramatic one.[10]

Three other writers of "tradiciones" are almost completely unknown because their output is small and because their "tradiciones" were published only in newspapers and magazines. These writers, Manuel Atanasio Fuentes, Aureliano Villarán and Marco A. de la Fuente, were contemporaries of Ricardo Palma. The first two published "'tradiciones" in *La Broma* during the same period in which Palma published many of his pieces in the same periodical. The third, Marco A. de la Fuente, was one of Palma's friends and carried on a sporadic correspondence with him. He even wrote one "tradición" entitled "Don Ricardo Palma 'tradicionado' " in which Palma appears as a principal figure.[11]

The name of Ricardo Palma was prominent in Peru because of his literary, newspaper, and political activities and because of his position as director of the National Library, which he created from nothing. It seemed that everyone in Peru who was involved in the world of letters and who lived during Palma's lifetime came into contact with him at one time or another. Perhaps more noteworthy is the fact that his reputation was an international one. His "tradiciones" and his poetry were printed in newspapers and magazines in all parts of the Hispanic world. His friends in other countries were legion; we can see in his correspondence that he was well acquainted with important literary figures in many parts of the globe. These bonds of friendship helped Palma to keep abreast of what was happening in the literature of other nations; they also made it possible for him to fill the shelves of the National Library with books he begged from friends and governments. When his *Tradiciones* appeared in published collections they were given a warm reception and succeeding series were eagerly awaited. A careful perusal of Peruvian newspapers and magazines printed during the last quarter of the nineteenth century gives the impression that

Palma wasn't just another writer; his figure took on major proportions. From the standpoint of his place in the Spanish American world of letters of the nineteenth century he would have to be considered one of the outstanding writers. His achievements and his popularity were such that his name might well be placed alongside those of writers of the stature of Rubén Darío, José Martí, and José Hernández.

But in the final analysis the figure of Ricardo Palma still looms large in Spanish American literature because he preserved Peru's past in delightful narratives which he called "tradiciones," a new type of literature which he invented. Many writers attempted to write "tradiciones" of their own, but their imitations fell short of the mark, primarily because Palma's style was unique; their own seemed lifeless and colorless when compared with his. Because of Ricardo Palma, Peru, and especially Lima, will live forever. His *Tradiciones,* which can be read by anyone who reads Spanish, are the door to a fascinating world which Palma has portrayed with unusual skill and verve.

Notes and References

Chapter One

1. *La literatura peruana* (Buenos Aires: Guaranía, 1950–1951), 6:215.
2. "Palma romántico" in *Tres ensayos sobre Ricardo Palma* (Lima, 1954), p. 21.
3. Ibid., p. 23.
4. César Miró, *Don Ricardo Palma: El Patriarca de las Tradiciones* (Buenos Aires, 1953), p. 31.
5. "El fraile y la monja," in *Tradiciones peruanas completas*, p. 1035.
6. "Consolación," in *Tradiciones peruanas completas*, p. 1164, note.
7. *Tradiciones peruanas completas*, p. 23, note.
8. George W. Umphrey and Carlos García Prada, "Introducción," in Ricardo Palma, *Flor de Tradiciones*, ed. George W. Umphrey and Carlos García Prada (Mexico City, 1943), p. ix.
9. "La bohemia de mi tiempo," p. 1297.
10. "Anales de la Inquisición de Lima," in *Tradiciones peruanas completas*, p. 1207.
11. "La estada en Chile," in *Tradiciones peruanas completas*, p. xxxvii. Miró (p. 74) gives the date as early in 1863.
12. Miró believes that Palma did not go to Para. See Miró, p. 80. José Miguel Oviedo, *Genio y figura de Ricardo Palma* (Buenos Aires, 1965), p. 71, suggests that Palma was in the Brazilian city twice, but for very brief periods of time.
13. Miró, p. 106.
14. *Epistolario*, ed. Raúl Porras Barrenechea (Lima, 1949), 1:55.
15. Ibid., 1:57.
16. *Obras selectas* (Madrid, 1958), pp. 1068–70, note 1.

Chapter Two

1. Ventura García Calderón, *Del romanticismo al modernismo* (París, 1910), p. 322.
2. *Cachivaches* (Lima, 1900), pp. 140–41.

3. "Libro nuevo," in Clorinda Matto de Turner, *Tradiciones cuzqueñas* (Lima, 1886), 2: xvii, xix.

4. Juan Valera, "Tradiciones peruanas," in *Cartas Americanas*, Vol. XLII of *Obras completas* (Madrid: Imprenta Alemana, 1915), p. 291.

5. See José Miguel Oviedo, *Genio y figura de Ricardo Palma* (Buenos Aires, 1965), p. 104.

6. *Cachivaches*, p. 142.

7. Ibid., p. 141.

8. "Cháchara," in Ricardo Palma, *Tradiciones peruanas completas*, p. 4.

9. *Epistolario*, ed. Raúl Porras Barrenechea (Lima, 1949), 1:333.

10. Ibid., p. 20.

11. Ibid., p. 334.

12. *Cachivaches*, p. 139.

13. Ibid., p. 141.

14. Guillermo Feliú Cruz, *La estancia en Chile*, Vol. 1 of *En torno de Ricardo Palma* (Santiago de Chile, 1933), pp. 332, 340.

15. Ibid., pp. 10, 28.

16. Raúl Porras Barrenechea, "Reseña cultural," in Ricardo Palma, *Tradiciones peruanas*, Vol. 25 of *Colección panamericana* (Buenos Aires, 1946), p. xliii.

17. Ricardo Palma, "Libro nuevo," in Clorinda Matto de Turner's *Tradiciones cuzqueñas* (Lima, 1886), p. xix.

18. Porras Barrenechea, p. l.

19. *Panorama de la littérature hispano-americaine* (Paris: Editions KRA, 1930), p. 225.

20. Feliú Cruz, p. 18.

Chapter Three

1. The earliest version I have been able to locate is found in *Revista de Buenos Aires*, April 1864, pp. 573–83.

2. Both "Lida" and "Mauro Cordato" (the "tradición" written shortly after "Lida"), were published by Juan Miguel Bakula Patiño in his *Don Ricardo Palma en Colombia: Tres de sus primeros impresos*, reprint of *Fénix* 12 (1958).

3. See Luis Hernán Ramírez, "*El estilo de las primeras tradiciones de Palma*" (Lima: Universidad Nacional de San Marcos, separata de *Sphinx* 14 [1961]: 5. The copy I have is found in *Revista Nacional* (Buenos Aires) 33 (1902): 282–86.

4. Guillermo Feliú Cruz, *La estancia en Chile*, Vol. 1 of *En torno de Ricardo Palma* (Santiago de Chile, Universidad de Chile, 1933), p. 214.

5. Ibid., p. 215.
6. See Ramírez, p. 5.
7. Pp. 266–70.
8. See William Wilder, "The Romantic Elements in the First Edition of the First Series of the *Tradiciones peruanas* by Ricardo Palma," Diss. St. Louis University, 1966, p. 101. Díaz Falconí says the date of publication was 1860, not 1861, the date used by Wilder. See Ramírez, p. 5.
9. Ibid., p. 90.

Chapter Four

1. *Del romanticismo al modernismo* (Paris, 1910), p. 328.
2. Merlin D. Compton, "Spanish Honor in Ricardo Palma's *Tradiciones peruanas*," Diss. University of California, Los Angeles, 1959, p. 232.
3. *Tradiciones peruanas completas*, p. 210.
4. Ibid.

Chapter Five

1. *Poesías completas* (Barcelona, 1911). There is some confusion about the publication dates of some of the collections in this volume. The dates provided in it do not agree with those provided by Edith Palma in *Tradiciones peruanas completas* or by Feliú Cruz in his *En torno de Ricardo Palma*.
2. "Poesías olvidadas de Ricardo Palma," *Sphinx* 15 (1962): 150.
3. *El Comercio*, August 31, 1848.
4. Ibid., November 25, 1848.
5. See Raúl Porras Barrenechea, "Palma romántico" in *Tres ensayos sobre Ricardo Palma* (Lima, 1954), pp. 24, 25.
6. *El Comercio*, August 29, 1850. My source for this information is *Ricardo Palma, autor teatral*, by Guillermo Ugarte Chamorro (Lima: Universidad de San Marcos, separata de *San Marcos* 14 [January-March 1976]): 137.
7. My source is Tauro, "Poesías olvidadas de Ricardo Palma" in *Sphinx* 15 (1962): 170. The poem was originally printed in *El Intérprete del Pueblo*, May 10–15, 1852.
8. Tauro, p. 165.
9. Ugarte Chamorro, pp. 140, 141.
10. Tauro, p. 202.
11. The date for *Juvenilia* is taken from *Poesías completas*, p. 8. The dates for *Armonías* and *Pasionarias* are found in *Tradiciones peruanas completas*, p. 1750.

12. *Poesías completas*, pp. 19–21.

13. Rubén Darío, *Obras completas* (Madrid: Afrodisio Aguado, 1950), 2:19.

14. *Poesías completas* (Barcelona, 1911) gives the following dates: *Verbos y gerundios*, 1878; *Nieblas*, 1906; and *Filigranas*, 1908. The dates given in *Tradiciones peruanas completas* are: *Verbos y gerundios*, 1877; *Nieblas*, 1887; and *Filigranas*, 1892. (See pp. 1750, 1751 in *Tradiciones peruanas completas*.)

15. See *Poesías completas*, p. 173.

16. Ibid., pp. 200, 201.

17. Ricardo Palma, *Epistolario*, ed. Raúl Porras Barrenechea (Lima, 1949), 1:28–29.

18. Ibid., pp. 417–18.

19. Ibid., p. 587.

Chapter Six

1. José Toribio Medina, "Prólogo," in Aurelio Díaz Meza, *Leyendas y episodios chilenos* (Buenos Aires, 1968), 1:1–2.

2. Ricardo Palma, *Epistolario*, ed. Raúl Porras Barrenechea (Lima, 1949), 1:125.

3. Ibid., p. 126.

4. Medina, p. 3, and Clemente Palma, "La tradición, los tradicionistas y las cosas de don Ricardo Palma, in *Don Ricardo Palma—1833–1933* (Lima, 1934), p. 221.

5. Clemente Palma, p. 222.

6. Medina, p. 4.

7. Ibid., p. 5.

8. Clemente Palma, p. 224.

9. Díaz Meza, 1:12.

10. Luis Alberto Sánchez, *La literatura peruana* (Buenos Aires: Guaranía, 1950–1951), 6:215.

11. For information concerning these three writers of "tradiciones" along with other information about the "tradición" in Peru see *Tradiciones desconocidas*, ed. Estuardo Núñez (Lima, 1974). On p. 7 Núñez writes the following: "His [Palma's] "tradiciones" were imitated ... by writers of merit inside and outside of Peru, to the point that in the second half of the 19th century his influence or his impact becomes very extensive. At least fifty writers in Peru and another fifty in other countries followed in his footsteps with similar success."

Selected Bibliography

PRIMARY SOURCES

1. Poetry

Armonías: Libro de un desterrado. París: Librería de Ch. Bouret, 1865.
Filigranas. Lima: Imprenta Benito Gil, 1892.
"Palma romántico," Raúl Porras Barrenechea, in *Tres ensayos sobre Ricardo Palma.* Lima: Librería Mejía Baca, 1954. This work contains some of Palma's poetry I have not found elsewhere.
Pasionarias. Havre: Tipografía Alfonso Lemale, 1870.
Poesías. Lima: Imprenta Torres Aguirre, 1887.
Poesías completas. Barcelona: Maucci, 1911.
"Poesías olvidadas de Ricardo Palma," Alberto Tauro, in *Sphinx* 15 (1962): 150–203. This is the best source for Palma's early poetry.
Ricardo Palma, autor teatral. Edited by Guillermo Ugarte Chamorro. Lima: Universidad de San Marcos, separata de *San Marcos* 14 (January-March 1976): 137. Contains some interesting poetry related to Peruvian drama.
Verbos y gerundios. Lima: Benito Gil, 1877.

2. Prose

Anales de la Inquisición de Lima. Found in Ricardo Palma, *Tradiciones peruanas completas.* Edited by Edith Palma. 2d ed. Madrid: Aguilar, 1953, pp. 1205–90. First published in book form in Lima, 1863.
Apéndice a mis últimas Tradiciones peruanas. Barcelona: Maucci, 1911.
La bohemia de mi tiempo. Found in Ricardo Palma, *Tradiciones peruanas completas.* Edited by Edith Palma. 2d ed. Madrid: Aguilar, 1953, pp. 1293–1321. First published in *Poesías.* Lima: Imprenta Torres Aguirre, 1887.

Cachivaches. Lima: Imprenta Torres Aguirre, 1900.

Cartas inéditas de Ricardo Palma. Edited by Rubén Vargas Ugarte. Lima: Carlos Milla Batres, 1964.

Corona patriótica. Lima: Tipografía del Mensajero, 1853.

El Demonio de los Andes. New York: Imprenta "Las Novedades," 1883.

Epistolario. 2 vols. Edited by Raúl Porras Barrenechea. Lima: Editorial Cultura Antártica, 1949.

The Knights of the Cape. Translated by Harriet de Onís. New York: Alfred A. Knopf, 1945.

"Libro nuevo," in Clorinda Matto de Turner, *Tradiciones cuzqueñas.* Lima: Imprenta Torres Aguirre, 1886.

Mis últimas Tradiciones peruanas y Cachivachería. Barcelona: Maucci, 1906.

"Monteagudo y Sánchez Carrión." Found in *Cachivaches.* Lima: Imprenta Torres Aguirre, 1900. First published in *Documentos literarios del Perú.* Edited by Manuel Odriozola. Lima: Imprenta del Estado, 1877.

Neologismos y americanismos. Found in Ricardo Palma, *Tradiciones peruanas completas.* Edited by Edith Palma. 2d ed. Madrid: Aguilar, 1953, pp. 1377–1408. First published in book form in Lima: Imprenta y Librería de Carlos Prince, 1896.

Papeletas lexicográficas. Dos mil setecientas voces que hacen falta en el Diccionario. Lima: Imprenta "La Industria," 1903.

Perú. Tradiciones. 1st Series. 2d ed. Lima: Imprenta del Universo, de Carlos Prince, 1883.

Perú. Tradiciones. 2nd Series. 2d ed. Lima: Imprenta del Universo, de Carlos Prince, 1883.

Perú. Tradiciones. 3rd Series. 2d ed. Lima: Imprenta del Universo, de Carlos Prince, 1883.

Perú. Tradiciones. 4th Series. 2d ed. Lima: Imprenta del Universo, de Carlos Prince, 1883.

Perú. Tradiciones. 5th Series. 1st ed. Lima: Imprenta del Universo, de Carlos Prince, 1883.

Perú. Tradiciones. 6th Series. 1st ed. Lima: Imprenta del Universo, de Carlos Prince, 1883.

Recuerdos de España. Found in Ricardo Palma, *Tradiciones peruanas completas.* Edited by Edith Palma. 2d ed. Madrid: Aguilar, 1953, pp. 1323–76. First published in book form in Lima, 1897.

Tradiciones. 1st Series. 1st ed. Lima: Imprenta del Estado, 1872.

Tradiciones. 2nd Series. 1st ed. Lima: Imprenta Liberal de "El Correo del Perú," 1874.

Tradiciones. 3rd Series. 1st ed. Lima: Benito Gil, 1877.

Tradiciones. 4th Series. 1st ed. Buenos Aires: Benito Gil, 1877.

Tradiciones. 1st Series. Buenos Aires: Klingelfuss, 1891.

Tradiciones en salsa roja. Pamphlet in the National Library of Lima.

Tradiciones en salsa verde. Typewritten copy in Duke University Library, Durham, North Carolina. A photostatic copy of this work is found in the National Library in Lima.

Tradiciones. Ropa apolillada. 8th Series. 1st ed. Lima: Imprenta del Universo, de Carlos Prince, 1891.

Tradiciones Ropa vieja. 7th Series. 1st ed. Lima: Imprenta del Universo, de Carlos Prince, 1889.

Tradiciones peruanas. 4 vols. Barcelona: Montaner y Simón, 1893.

Tradiciones peruanas. 6 vols. Madrid: Espasa-Calpe, 1923. Later editions were published in 1945–1947 and 1966. All editions were published under the auspices of the Peruvian government.

Tradiciones peruanas. 6 vols. Edited by Raúl Porras Barrenechea. Lima: Editorial Cultura Antártica, 1951.

Tradiciones peruanas completas. Edited by Edith Palma. Madrid: Aguilar, 1952. Later editions were published in 1953, 1957, and 1964.

Tradiciones selectas del Perú. 2 vols. Callao: A.J. Segrestán y Cía., 1911.

Tradiciones y artículos históricos. Lima: Imprenta Torres Aguirre, 1899.

SECONDARY SOURCES

Bákula Patiño, Juan Miguel. "Don Ricardo Palma en Colombia. Tres de sus primeros impresos." *Fénix* (Lima) 12 (1958): 78–141. A very valuable addition to Palma's works which contains two of Palma's early pieces, "Lida" and "Mauro Cordato," together with the history of the two narratives and their reworked versions. Bákula Patiño also compares the original versions with the others.

Bazán, Dora. "El personaje femenino en las *Tradiciones peruanas.*" *Sphinx* (Lima), 2a época, 14 (1961): 156–77. A perceptive introductory study of women in the "tradiciones." One of her conclusions is that women appear less frequently in the later pieces.

Bazin, Robert. "Les trois crises de la vie de Ricardo Palma." *Bulletin Hispanique* 56, no. 1–2 (1954): 49–82. Discussion of three critical points in Palma's life. They are (1) his disillusionment after the murder of President Balta; (2) the Monteagudo-Sánchez Carrión polemic; and (3) attacks by González Prada on Palma as a "do-nothing" conservative.

Caillet-Bois, Julio. "Problemas de lengua y estilo en las *Tradiciones peruanas.*" *Revista de la Universidad de la Plata* 3 (January-March 1958): 69–79. A brief discussion of the nature and development of the "tradición." One of the few treatments of the evolution of the "tradición" in which the primitive pieces are considered.

Compton, Merlin D. "Las *Tradiciones peruanas* de Ricardo Palma: Bibliografía y lista cronológica tentativas." *Duquesne Hispanic Review* 8, no. 3 (Spring 1969): 1–24. Needs some updating but is a valuable tool for placing the "tradiciones" in the order in which they were written.

Don Ricardo Palma 1833–1933. Lima: Sociedad de Amigos de Palma, 1934. An outstanding series of studies published on the centenary of Palma's birth. Authors include Raúl Porras Barrenechea, Víctor Andrés Belaúnde, José Gálvez, Angélica Palma, Clemente Palma, and José de la Riva Agüero. Also contains some of Palma's letters and other materials.

Escobar, Alberto. "Tensión, lenguaje y estructura: Las *Tradiciones peruanas.*" *Anejo de Sphinx* 15, no. 6 (1962): 9–55. A detailed comparison of an early "tradición" with its later version. Escobar notes major changes in the second version and points out that when Palma wrote his mature pieces he abandoned a tragic somberness for a "smiling irony" and created a language which caused greater artistic tension. Indispensable for a study of Palma's style.

Feliú Cruz, Guillermo. *En torno de Ricardo Palma.* Vol. 1: *La estancia en Chile:* Vol. 2 *Ensayo crítico-bibliográfico.* Santiago: Universidad de Chile, 1933. Well-documented study of Palma's stay in Chile and his development as a writer of "tradiciones." This work also contains a detailed bibliography of Palma's works until 1933, the best one of its kind.

García Calderón, Ventura. *Del romanticismo al modernismo.* París: Sociedad de Ediciones Literarias y Artísticas, [1910]. Critical appraisal of Palma and his "tradiciones" by a Peruvian writer. Incisive and studded with worthwhile insights.

Martinengo, Alessandro. *Lo stile di Ricardo Palma.* Padua: Liviana, 1962. Valuable study of Palma's style. Especially interesting is his focus on the *Anales de la Inquisición.*

Miró, Cesar. *Don Ricardo Palma: El patriarca de las Tradiciones.* Buenos Aires: Losada, 1953. One of the basic biographies on Ricardo Palma. Interweaves material from the "tradiciones" with Palma's life.

Oviedo, José Miguel. *Genio y figura de Ricardo Palma.* Buenos Aires: Eudeba, 1965. An in-depth study of the life and the works of Palma. Indispensable.

Palma, Angélica. *Ricardo Palma.* Buenos Aires: Cóndor, 1933. The first of the Palma biographies and one of the best. Angélica was Ricardo's daughter and she provides biographical material, anecdotes, and personal observations about her father.

Ramírez, Luis Hernán. "El estilo de las primeras tradiciones de Palma." *Sphinx* 2a separata época, no. 14 (1961): 126–55. Another of the fundamental studies of Palma's style. Ramírez studies the style of the definitive edition of the First Series and, although it differs from the original (1872) edition of that series, many of the early "tradiciones" are analyzed with great care. Some of his conclusions are too subjective but his study as a whole breaks fresh ground in the analysis of some of Palma's early attempts.

Salomon, Noël. "Las orejas del alcalde de Ricardo Palma: Un exemple de fabrication littéraire." *Bulletin Hispanique* 69 (1967): 441–53. Salomon extracts an incident from a historical work with which Palma was acquainted and hypothesizes that he created a "tradición" from it. The differences between the incident and the "tradición" are very revealing.

Umphrey, George W., and García Prada, Carlos. "Introducción," in Ricardo Palma, *Flor de Tradiciones*. Edited by George W. Umphrey and Carlos García Prada. Mexico City: Editorial Cultura, 1943. A good short portrayal of Palma and his works.

Wilder, William R. "The Romantic Elements in the First Edition of the First Series of the 'Tradiciones peruanas.' " Diss. St. Louis University 1966. Although this dissertation appears to be very restricted the author has provided much valuable information about Palma's relationship to Romanticism and his early years when he was trying to find his way. The study is especially valuable because Wilder treats some "tradiciones" which were part of the 1872 edition but have since been eliminated and are now very difficult to locate. He also includes "La querida del pirata" in complete form, an early "tradición" Palma excluded from his definitive edition of "tradiciones."

Index